Panzer

Panzer

Philip Warner

Arthur Barker Limited

Designed by John Rushton Associates
for Arthur Barker Limited

Printed in Great Britain by
Cox & Wyman Ltd,
London, Fakenham and Reading

Colour Separations by
Radstock Reproductions

Contents

1 The Panzer

Pioneers

The Second World War endowed many simple words and phrases with a significance well beyond the original meaning. This phenomenon was owing to the overwhelming effect that certain weapons or tactics had at one stage or other during the war. 'U boats', already a chilling term from the First World War, became a symbol of naval destruction in 1943. 'Spitfire' was a word to make any German airman thoughtful in 1940, and B29 (B *Ni ju ku*), the American heavy bomber, was a portent of doom to the Japanese in 1944. There were many others which those living through that time will recall with vivid clarity. In such a list the word 'Panzer' will invariably appear. To the Germans 'Panzer' is simply 'armour' and is used to make up compound words such as *Panzergruppe* (armoured unit), *Panzerjäger* (anti-tank troops) and *Panzerkampfwagen* (armoured fighting vehicle). Panzer became a general term to describe armoured units just as the Allies used 'armour' to describe the whole range of fighting vehicles. However, outside the German forces the word Panzer had an awesome mystique quite out of proportion to its potential. This appears to have been acquired in Poland in 1939 and in Western Europe in 1940 and 1941. Even when the Panzers had run into serious trouble in the Middle East and Russia and were being outclassed and destroyed the word still kept its prestige. During and after the Second World War there can have been very few people in the nations fighting Germany who did not know the significance of the word Panzer. In the German forces the term PzKw was used – an abbreviation of *Panzerkampfwagen*. The Germans and Russians are less addicted to giving their weapons nicknames than Western nations are, although it sometimes happens. Thus, the Russians had T34s and the Germans PzKw IVs, while the Allies had Churchills and Shermans and Matildas and Crusaders. Often the Allies would find an appropriate nickname

PREVIOUS PAGES An English tank halted at Cambrai, 1917. The tank's potential as a weapon interested the Germans but its many drawbacks made them cautious.

BELOW In 1917 the English tried to break right through the German front line at Cambrai. Initial success was not exploited after the loss of 300 tanks. Here, intrigued German soldiers inspect one.

for a weapon the Germans had designed to be the very symbol of terror. From this strange sense of humour came the name 'Big Bertha' for the huge Krupp gun of the First World War and 'Doodlebug' for the destructive rockets of the Second World War. Panzers never acquired a nickname. Even to those who fought and destroyed them the word had an emotional overtone which could not be altered. There was something enigmatic about Panzers; they came rapidly to fame and then after a period of glory were eclipsed. Their ultimate failure was as mysterious as their origins.

Mysterious indeed those origins had to be. At the end of the First World War the Treaty of Versailles had decreed that the German army should be limited to 100,000 and forbidden the use of military aircraft. The newly-formed state of Soviet Russia had allowed the Germans facilities for training pilots secretly (a training the Russians would later have cause to regret) but for armoured vehicles the Germans at first had to rely on their own ingenuity, which was considerable.

Panzer development in Germany had to face many more difficulties than evading the provisions of the Versailles Treaty. The Higher Command of the attenuated German army of the 1920s was by no means unanimously convinced of the value of the tank as a weapon. In 1916 and 1917 the Germans had been surprised by the advent of the tank and its potential but the obvious limitations of the new weapon, which varied from the internal mechanical problems to the external ones of terrain and enemy firepower, had given force to the arguments of those who believed that the best weapons and methods of war were those which they themselves had learned when young officers, perhaps twenty years earlier. There is no space here to go into the oddities of military conservatism but in every century and in every country there had been a hard core of conservative resistance to military innovation. In the last century the attitude seems in part to have stemmed from a desperate desire to preserve the privilege of horsed cavalry long after the machine-gun had sealed the fate of mounted troops.

In Germany there were two minds actively considering the possibilities of armoured warfare even as early as 1922. One was General Hans von Seeckt, who was Commander-in-Chief between 1920 and 1926. Like Count Alfred von Schlieffen who designed the strategy of the German attack in 1914 but died before it was launched, von Seeckt also died before the outbreak of the war for which he had planned. Von Seeckt's studies of military history had given him an intense admiration of Friedrich Seydlitz who had achieved great victories in the eighteenth century by surprise, speed and encircling movements and flank attacks. Seeckt visualized that if the Panzer could be made fast, mobile and reliable, twentieth-century warfare could be concluded as successfully as Seydlitz's campaigns. The Russians now offered facilities for the Reichswehr (Germany's army) to experiment in defiance of the Versailles Treaty, another policy which they had cause to regret in 1941. The Swedes too were co-operative. In 1922 a young captain named Heinz Guderian was given a staff appointment in the transport division of the Reichswehr and soon drew attention to himself by writing articles in the army journal on the possible uses of armoured vehicles. Soon there was beginning to develop a nucleus of thinkers who were firmly convinced that the methods of the First World War, slow, costly and frustrating, could be replaced by a relatively cheap, rapid and exciting form of warfare. The members of the German army in the 1920s were all highly professional, both officers and men. There was much experience of victory and defeat and being a small, closely-knit band, they were able to experiment and train with an enthusiasm which would have been lacking with greater numbers. At this time the Germans used mock tanks fashioned with cardboard superstructures. Observers from other countries who heard of these extraordinary improvisations laughed derisively. The long-term results were, however, anything but laughable for Germany's future opponents. The cardboard models gave useful lessons in the possibilities of inter-unit co-operation and also furnished a legend that

RIGHT Because the Versailles Treaty restricted rearmament, Germany initially sated its curiosity about tanks by experimenting with mock ones in the 1920s.

BELOW Although Germany's mock tanks amused the rest of Europe, the trials continued through the early 1930s and taught the Germans that this source of amusement would prove a formidable weapon.

German rearmament – when it was racing ahead in the 1930s – was futile and could be ignored for their tanks were only made of cardboard.

In 1938 when the Nazis occupied Austria there was a widely believed story that an English tourist with an ancient Austin car had collided with a German tank. The tank, it was said, had crumpled on impact and turned out to be made of cardboard. It was a comforting little story for those opposing British rearmament but it had a hollow ring to those British servicemen trying to stop German tanks in 1940 and finding their bullets merely bouncing off the armour.

In the early days, progress was not nearly as rapid or smooth as the protagonists of tank warfare would have liked. There were few officers with the experience and single-mindedness of Guderian. Before he turned his attention to armoured vehicles Guderian had been an infantry officer, a staff officer and a signals officer. In the last appointment he made a sound appreciation of what was required for control and intercommunication on the battlefield. In the 1920s, the means at his disposal were primitive by later standards but they sufficed for him to make correct assessments.

Any innovation, whether in a military or civilian sphere, tends to be regarded with caution and an element of distrust. In the army a new weapon or tactic is likely to produce a variety of reactions. Those to whose arm it is particularly suitable will regard it with warmth, others may regard it as possibly adaptable to their own requirements and yet others will regard it with frank hostility. When the tank had established itself by the battle of Cambrai in 1917, cavalrymen, who knew that their beloved horses had no future on the battlefield, welcomed this new form of cavalry weapon. Admittedly it was noisy, smelly, undignified and unreliable, but it had great potential and, best of all, it meant a future for cavalry regiments which would otherwise have been converted to other arms. The general reaction of the Higher Command, therefore, tended to be favourable for there are few higher commands where former cavalry officers are not influential. However, when the full implications of Guderian's idea began to be known there was considerable opposition. Guderian saw the tank as the dominant factor on the battlefield. It was not to be relegated to a reconnaissance vehicle for infantry and under infantry command or subject to the whims of artillery commanders. He wrote, 'Tanks must play the primary role, the other weapons being subordinated to the requirements of the armour ... tanks will never be able to produce their full effect until the other weapons on whose support they must inevitably rely are brought up to the same standard of speed and cross-country performance.' These were strong words. Tanks might have been cumbersome and slow but they were fleet compared with some of the guns on which they might have to rely for support. Nor was the idea of being subordinate to tanks a role likely to commend itself to élite infantry formations. They saw the tank as their subordinate. Ironically, Guderian's ideas owed much to the writings of two British military theorists, B. H. Liddell-Hart and J. F. C. Fuller. Both of these men visualized the need for the tank to be given the primary role with the support of other arms but, as is sadly known, neither succeeded in obtaining support for these ideas in Britain. Instead the Germans, among others, appreciated and applied their theories. Thus, in 1940, Britain was far behind in a theory of warfare in which she had been the pioneer. Guderian was lucky that in 1923 Walter von Brauchitsch, later to be Commander-in-Chief, tried out some of Guderian's ideas on that year's manoeuvres. He was less lucky in 1929 when his new commanding officer, General Karl von Stülpnagel, flatly forbade any further experiments in what he believed was a thoroughly impractical form of warfare. Guderian was lucky again in 1931 when von Stülpnagel was replaced by Oswald Lutz who believed firmly in Guderian's ideas and appointed him his Chief of Staff. The obstacles were by no means overcome but from now onwards progress would be so rapid that in 1939 Germany would astonish the world. When in 1933 Hitler had firmly established himself in power he appointed Werner von Blomberg as Minister of War. Blomberg knew that Hitler was determined to build a new

Panzer Protagonists

In the 1920s men like von Seeckt (far left) and Guderian (left) initiated the endless debates concerning the practicality of tanks in warfare; others who favoured tank development included: Walter von Brauchitsch (below left), seen with Admiral Raeder; Adolf Hitler (far right), photographed with von Blomberg (centre) and von Fritsch; and, in the photograph in the lower right corner, von Bock (left) and von Reichenau.

army with ideas far in advance of those which had only produced slaughter and defeat in 1918. The new Panzer theories seemed ideally suited to their requirements and another significant appointment, that of General Walter von Reichenau to the post of Chief of Ministerial Office, gave yet another vigorous thinker his opportunity. Von Reichenau and Guderian became firm friends as they worked for the common objective.

By 1931 the Germans had assembled a useful dossier of information on the possibilities of armoured vehicles. Much of this came from Berlin, for in addition to the writings of Liddell-Hart and Fuller there was a very useful report on the Experimental Mechanized Force exercises which had been held in 1927 and 1928. There was no serious attempt to keep this document secret and soon it was being studied more actively in Germany than in Britain. (It was mentioned in the spy trial of Capt. Baillie-Stewart as being supplied by him to the Germans.) What neither Britain nor anyone else outside Germany knew was that in 1926 the German army had ordered and taken delivery of two tanks, one of 9 tons and one of 20 tons. Had this flagrant disavowal of the treaty become known, though, it seems unlikely that anyone would have paid much attention to it.

The fact that Hitler's assumption of supreme power in 1933 cleared the way for the development of Panzers did not mean that Panzer troubles were now over; in fact they were only just beginning. The problem of Hitler's interference in strategy and tactics belonged to the future; for the moment there were three other problems. One was the Versailles Treaty, which would gradually be repudiated (in 1935); the second was the lack of a tank which would do all that was expected of it; and the third was the provision of suitably trained tank crews. They would be solved in that order but, as with aircraft, it soon became apparent that the design and production of machines was infinitely simpler than finding and training the right quality crews to man them. The supply of men and materials was, surprisingly enough, given no special priority. Even when General Werner von Fritsch was made Commander-in-Chief of the Army in 1934 and General Oswald Lutz made General of Panzer Troops the following year, the Panzers received no special privileges. Their usefulness was not denied by their comrades in arms but when it came to giving them an extra share of money, materials and men – that was a different story. Guderian himself was given command of the 2nd Panzer regiment. This undoubtedly provided him with valuable experience but it had the frustrating disadvantage of removing him from the planning area where his foresight, persuasion and experience could be most effective, for by this time the tank had shown that it was perhaps the most difficult of all battle weapons to assess.

Should tanks be heavily armoured and therefore made nearly invulnerable although very slow? Should they on the other hand have light armour but devastating guns so that they could demolish opposition at long range, again at the expense of speed? Should they perhaps sacrifice almost everything to speed and manoeuvrability, relying on speed to disconcert the enemy and throw him off balance, or mobility to extricate themselves from situations which had suddenly become intolerable? All being well there would be tanks of all types: fast light reconnaissance tanks; medium tanks which could pour through gaps in what has poetically been described by Fuller as 'an expanding torrent'; and heavy tanks which could lumber up and by slogging it out toe-to-toe demolish fortifications while the lighter brethren stood on one side. One thing was certain; nothing would ever be perfect. Anti-tank weapons, guns or mines, would be developed which would upset all the tank men's calculations; tanks, though very effective with air support, would seem exceptionally vulnerable to air attack themselves; mechanical troubles would seem endless. Clearly the most vulnerable part of a tank was the track and once a track was damaged a tank became a sitting target. Bullets which entered tanks had an uncomfortable habit of ricocheting around doing damage as they went. Ammunition in tanks would sometimes explode spontaneously from a variety of causes. Crews could

be overcome by heat or fumes or even sea-sickness when the tank travelled too quickly over rough ground. To this day there is much controversy over what is the maximum speed for a tank. Tanks appear very formidable, perhaps invincible, as they lumber towards you with guns smoking, but the history of tank warfare is full of instances of brave, near-suicidal men destroying tanks by diving under them with explosives or pouring petrol on to the turrets and setting them alight. As with aircraft, a decision sometimes has to be made whether the time is ripe for the mass production of a certain model. Are armour, firepower and speed likely to be effective for the next few years? The mass production of a tank or an aircraft is not likely to take less than a few years from the laying down of the production line to the use of the finished products with their inevitable modifications. If the decision is taken just before some new development in armour or gunnery, a nation may be saddled with thousands of obsolete tanks. The effect on morale is incalculable. On the other hand, the possession of the best tank in the world is of little use if there are not enough of them at the right time. Plentiful supplies of obsolescent tanks are not to be despised; they will not all be destroyed and the ones which get through will do much damage.

The problems of tank warfare were not limited to the tank itself. The most obvious requirement is fuel and a vast army of tanks needs enormous quantities of it. That factor alone was going to prove a serious limitation to Germany's Panzer development. Infantry can be exercised at low cost; tank training demands large quantities of fuel. Once tanks are launched in an attack it is vital that they should be adequately supplied; if supplies break down tanks are merely being presented to the enemy. As will be seen later, when the Germans made their deep long thrusts into enemy territory, the policy appeared to many,

OPPOSITE German light reconnaissance tanks at Aalt

ABOVE German tank with a badly damaged track at Tschertkowo in 1942.

Half-track personnel carriers were vital to the Panzer units; this one was photographed in 1942 in the Ukraine.

both Germans and Allies, to be reckless to the point of suicide. It appeared that they must have outrun fuel supplies, ammunition supplies and maintenance sections. Tank crews need food just like other soldiers and although the Panzer crews had burning enthusiasm and high morale this did not mean they were immune to fatigue. Tanks, too, have the same limitations as horsed cavalry; they cannot on their own hold ground. For this they need infantry. In the conditions of the Second World War infantry could not be moved very rapidly. In theory the problem of infantry keeping pace with Panzer units was partly solved by the creation of *Panzergrenadier* units which moved alongside in half-tracked personnel carriers (*Schützenpanzerwagen*), when these were available, or via lorries or motor cycles when they could follow the tanks, but availability of fuel and road conditions held up mechanical vehicles. The limits of Panzer strategy therefore depended on the extent to which all these slowing-down factors could be minimized.

An unfortunate characteristic of tanks is that if they travel along ordinary roads, as is preferable for greater speed, the effect on the surface is devastating. This is not so important if the road is merely to be used by other tanks but poses serious problems when the route is used by other vehicles, carrying urgently needed supplies. A road surface which has been torn up by tank tracks will soon let in enough rain to make it virtually impassable by other transportation.

In 1934 the Panzers could see the way ahead but it was a way beset by obstacles. Every development so far had been in the teeth of difficulties. The very existence of a tank in the German armed forces had been prohibited by the Versailles Treaty but the prohibition had been circumvented. The first proponents of tank warfare – Guderian, Lutz, von Reichenau – had at the time been so junior in rank and faced with such conservatism in their seniors that their efforts initially met little success. There were only four thousand officers in the entire Reichswehr, so promotion was frustratingly slow. The early experiments exposed the Panzer pioneers to ridicule which would have withered less dedicated men. At the time of apparent success, in 1929, when further progress first seemed assured, all progress was stopped. At the moment when Guderian seemed in a position to make positive plans for the extension of the Panzer force, he was suddenly transferred to a regimental post. Over all there was the desperate competition for scarce materials and, what is always scarcer, first-class men. All this was done in the 1920s against a national background of runaway inflation, economic chaos, food shortages and general apathy. Small wonder that when the Panzer arm was finally created the Panzer pioneers appeared as steely

A self-propelled gun (*Sturmgeschütz*) of an SS division near Metz in May 1940

as the vehicles they commanded. Imbued with patriotism, and undeterred by any setback, they acquired a form of ruthless determination which has rarely been matched. Naturally, their opponents saw these qualities in a less favourable light than their own countrymen did, but when one considers the obstacles which were overcome even their opponents accord a grudging admiration. Ingenuity was the order of the day; on many fronts the Panzers were later out-numbered by their opponents and losses of materials were compensated for by tactics, improvisation and 'cannibalizing' damaged tanks.

At this point it is necessary to clarify distinctions such as that between a tank and a self-propelled gun. The self-propelled gun was called *Sturmgeschütz* (*Panzerjäger* were the troops manning anti-tank guns which were known as *PAK-Panzerabwehrkanone*). The *Sturmgeschütz* had a tank-chassis which carried a gun mounted without a turret. The gun could therefore not be moved in a 360° circle but only along an angle of approximately 20°. This meant that it had to be aimed by the driver, with the gunner zeroing in with his telescopic sight. The *Sturmgeschütz* presented a much lower silhouette than a tank and carried more firepower as the chassis did not have to bear a large and heavy turret and could therefore hold a bigger gun. Thus the chassis of a PZ IV could carry a Panther-gun (75 mm, super-long, high-velocity) while the Panther chassis held the 88 mm super-long of the *Königstiger*. *Flakpanzer* were designed for defending armoured columns against air attack; flak means anti-aircraft gunfire. *Funkwagen* were radio tanks or armoured cars used for communication work. *Minenraumpanzer* were for clearing mines and *Räumschaufelpanzer* were tanks equipped with shovels like bulldozers for clearance work. *Waffenträger* were weapon carriers, as were the *Selbstfahrlafetten*. *Panzerspähwagen* were fast armoured cars mainly used in reconnaissance.

In view of the fact that Germany and Russia eventually made more use of tanks than other nations it is interesting to remember that both derived most of their knowledge from the British Vickers Medium tank of 1923 (16 mph, range 150 miles, 47 mm gun, 6·5 mm armour) and the American Christie (30 mph. 9 tons, armament etc. varied).

Once a satisfactory basic design had been established there was endless scope for development of the component parts. Thickness of armour, power of armament and power of engine have been considered. There were now such matters as improved suspension and mobility, modification of gear boxes, tracks and steering. Tanks would never properly be proved until tested in war but for the moment peacetime trials were made as searching and realistic as possible.

ABOVE Recruitment poster for Goering's
Panzer Division.
RIGHT Panzers in a captured French
town, May 1940

2 The Birth of

1935

the Panzers,

ABOVE Infiltrating France, Panzers raced
from town to town with awesome speed
and indiscriminate destruction.

OPPOSITE A German soldier surveying
Panzer devastation in France

n March 1935 Hitler renounced the Versailles Treaty. The gesture gave great satisfaction in Germany but made little impact outside. Since 1919 there had been many liberal thinkers who had denounced the Treaty of Versailles as being too harsh. It had stripped Germany of her colonies and changed her frontiers; it had limited the size of her army and fixed a sum for reparations. The terms of the treaty were undoubtedly hard but as has been somewhat cynically observed they were not as bad as they would have been if Germany had faithfully observed them. We have already seen the evasion of the prohibition on tanks and military aircraft. The French, who had paid off proportionately heavier 'reparations' in 1871 after the Franco-Prussian war, pointed out that Germany made little effort to pay her full share of reparations after 1919. In the early stages they had been paid with borrowed money and in the later stages not paid at all. Other countries, such as Hungary and Austria, which had been subject to separate treaties, had in fact been penalized far more harshly than Germany. In the atmosphere of pacifism and appeasement of the 1930s the denunciation of a sixteen-year-old treaty, widely believed to be vindictively harsh, was unlikely to provoke a strong reaction – as Hitler knew. At the same time he announced that conscription would be reintroduced into Germany. America had no wish to be involved in European affairs and was determined not to be 'dragged in'. Britain and France were too much concerned with the antics of Mussolini to be able to give Hitler the attention his words and deeds merited. And there were other worries, too. The Japanese were becoming powerful and truculent in the Far East and the Russians were building tanks at an astonishing pace. Real danger from Germany was discounted by her neighbours; even in 1936 when Hitler reoccupied the Rhineland there was no strong reaction. Outside Germany there was a general feeling that all that was happening was that unilaterally Germany was rectifying a few injustices. Rumours of less pleasant activities and philosophies were discounted or ignored. There was a new government and a new spirit in Germany and it boded ill for Germany's neighbours as they would later discover; but for the moment most people refused to face unpleasant facts. Thus it remained for four years. In those four years the Panzers were born.

In the German army there were two types of conflict. Some German generals approved of Hitler; others did not. As Hitler approved of the Panzers those who did not care for the man whom they saw as an Austrian upstart and demagogue tried to place as many obstacles in the way of Panzers as they could without retarding the development of the German army. This, therefore, created one type of planning conflict. The second clash was the one mentioned before – whether the infantry should control the tanks or whether the tanks should dominate the infantry and other arms. Ultimately a satisfactory compromise was reached. Tanks were concentrated in armoured divisions but the infantry controlled motorized divisions. The cavalry took over motorized reconnaissance.

The first test of the new tanks came in Spain. Civil War had begun in the summer of 1936. The Government side was Republican and Russian-backed; the insurgents under General Franco were anti-Communist and were backed by Germany and Italy, both of which were Fascist. Britain spent much time ineffectually trying to organize non-intervention and both sides in Spain had British volunteers fighting for them, though in small numbers. The Italians supplied light carriers and the Germans sent PzKpfw Is. The PzKpfw I was a light tank weighing only 5·5 tons, with a speed of 22 mph, carrying a crew of two, protected by 12 mm armour and carrying two machine-guns. The lack of a heavy gun made it more of a carrier than a tank but it was capable of considerable development and was eventually widely used. It looked more formidable than it was but that information would be of scant use to opponents lacking adequate anti-tank weapons. However, tank warfare cannot be waged by one type of tank only: the correct use of tanks involves three types, or tactical advantages may not be exploited.

PREVIOUS PAGES A Panzer parade, finale of the Nazi Congress at Nuremburg, 1936

The German contribution to tank warfare in Spain was limited by the unsuitability of the vehicles they dispatched. It was otherwise with the Russians. Not only did they send T27s but they also accompanied them with their best tank tacticians such as D. G. Pavlov and Konstantin Rokossovsky. The German commander was Colonel Wilhelm von Thoma. The opening battles soon showed the difference between theory and practice. It has been aptly said that once the first shot is fired there descends on the battlefield 'the fog of war'. The fog is one of mental confusion as commanders grapple with the problems of not only what the enemy is doing but what their own supporters are doing instead of what they were expected to be doing. The 'fog of war' descended promptly in Spain. First, at Esquivas, in October 1936, the Russians broke through but lost touch with their infantry and soon had to retire through lack of fuel. The following January the Germans broke through the Republican front but could not identify satisfactory targets and, in any case, also left their own infantry behind. It is not difficult to leave infantry behind in a tank battle for once the ironclads begin circling around each other, belching apparently indiscriminate destruction, the best motivated infantryman may feel a certain hesitation about advancing into the middle of it all. However, after some experience of tanks on the battlefield even the lowliest infantryman begins to form opinions on their correct use. He is prepared to accept the fact that in adequate numbers they are devastating (and well he might) but with an adequate anti-tank weapon he is personally prepared for isolated tanks. As far as his own army's tanks are concerned, he feels they should be allotted specific tasks such as reconnaissance and the destruction of enemy strong points. He will be glad of their assistance but views with distrust their claims to win battles on their own. In Spain the prevalence of the infantry-man's viewpoint caused Franco to put pressure on von Thoma to disperse his tanks among the infantry. This was resisted but otherwise von Thoma's experience and comments were of scant use to the cause which Guderian was so anxiously advocating. His conclusion was that the influence of the tank in battle had been much overrated and that the installation of radio in each tank, for which

German Condor Legion units (right) with Spanish nationalists (left) near the end of the Spanish Civil War

Panzers in Niš during the invasion of Yugoslavia.

Guderian had been pressing, was unnecessary. Guderian countered these arguments by saying that Spain was a false proving ground, for tanks were being used in areas for which they were not suited, such as city suburbs, the crews and their supporters were insufficiently trained and tanks had never been used in sufficient numbers. His persuasion, if not his arguments, gradually won the day and the German Panzer force was doubled to make it up to six divisions.

Guderian now had his Panzer force but there was still no certainty that he would be able to use it as he wished. General Ludwig Beck was the Chief of the Army General Staff from 1935 to 1938. Beck did not believe that warfare could be conducted as Guderian wished. Guderian wished to be in the front of the battle, controlling it by radio. Beck believed that a commander could not obtain a proper view of the battlefield if he were personally involved in it. The fact that Beck considered Guderian an impractical dreamer meant that the latter, in spite of being Chief of Mobile Troops, faced endless frustrations. The Panzers which urgently needed priority in supplies had to take their turn with older and better equipped arms. It may seem almost incredible today but in 1938 there was a strong school of thought throughout the German army that Guderian should not be given high command in wartime. Beck was replaced by Franz Halder in August 1938, and Halder retained this vital post till September 1942. Surprisingly enough, in spite of all the successes they gained, Halder was never sympathetic to the Panzers either. The pace of German rearmament was fast in the late 1930s. They were building submarines and cruisers, bombers and fighters, as well as making weapons of many types. The competition for materials and skilled labour was intense. In such circumstances everyone puts in a claim for more resources than he needs in the certain knowledge that his allotment will be less than his request and, indeed, than his needs. The Panzers were in this marketplace but their needs were urgent and genuine, while some of the others were not. In consequence, essential needs of the Panzers were not met but other arms received equipment which they could have managed without.

From the start it was obvious that AFVs (armoured fighting vehicles) of any type, whether light armoured cars or heavy tanks, were going to be constantly in need of spare parts. This was appreciated as far as their guns were concerned for the maintenance service are well aware of the ailments which can affect the performance of the sturdiest of guns; artillery has a long history. The problems connected with the armour, gearing, engines and suspension of tanks were largely unfamiliar. Ever since tanks have been used metallurgists have been urged to produce tougher but lighter armour. Frequently they were able to do so, but high-quality armour-plate presents its own problems. If it is in any way flawed, caused by minute and almost undetectable impurities, it is liable to shatter easily when struck by a shell. There can be no question of trial and error here. However, flawless high-quality steel is extremely difficult to use in manufacture and is very expensive. As in almost every manufacturing process there has been controversy between methods of construction (by riveting or welding) and between oxy-acetylene and electric welding. Riveting is very strong but the heads of rivets may sheer off if struck. Electric welding, which was used in Germany after 1934, was quicker and cheaper but could create problems from uneven cooling, which led to cracking. However it was generally found to be a satisfactory process. As may be imagined, each fresh development in manufacturing armour-plate brought a series of attendant problems. Not least of the problems of welding is the production of sufficient numbers of skilled welders. Welding two steel plates together is not unduly difficult but welding the inside of awkward corners or curves is a strain mentally as well as physically.

Modern tank drivers are usually amused to learn that the first tanks, which lumbered into action on the Western Front in 1916, had four men allotted to the task of steering and gear-changing. Steering in those days, and for some time afterwards, was based on the principle of disengaging the drive and applying the brake to one track. Clearly this would not have sufficed when tanks became

OPPOSITE Panzer production line

28

November 1941, at Matrenino, near Moscow, German soldiers light a fire in an attempt to free their tank from the ice.

faster for it would have resulted in them spinning around in circles. The most successful gearbox eventually proved to be the Maybach which was used not only in PzKws but also adapted for British use in the Churchill and many later tanks where it was called the Merritt-Brown box. The Maybach box was infinitely more complicated than the earlier boxes but had the advantage that it could be operated by one man without necessarily occupying his full attention.

Engines – or power plants as they are more usually known – began as water-cooled, bulky, petrol-driven units. Tank engines are required to perform under even more exacting conditions than aircraft engines, that is when tilted from the vertical, when subjected to extremes of temperature, when badly-maintained, when in clouds of dust or sand and when raced to maximum revs. They are also required to start easily, be economical on fuel and not be too noisy. An engine which produced exhaust smoke could ruin a surprise attack; it is not always easy to spot a camouflaged tank but an advancing plume of smoke is a different matter. Last but not least the engine must be easy to maintain in field conditions. The development of diesel engines removed a principal fire hazard, and air-cooling helped to reduce unwanted bulk.

Space inside a tank was always a subject of jealous competition. An ideal theoretical design, planned in a comfortable office, might not seem quite so attractive to a tank crew working in strenuous and uncomfortable battle positions. In theory one man could drive, and another one operate the gun and the radio; in practice it might be necessary to have a driver, a co-driver who

PzKw IV interior

could be an auxiliary gunner, a main gunner, a loader, a radio operator and a commander. Ultimately most countries found five men was the optimum, and the amount of space allotted to the crew, in relation to ammunition, fuel and other stores, had to bear relation to basic human needs such as comfort and fatigue. Such matters were usually the result of experience, and woe betide a tank whose technical excellence made it so cramped that its crew hated the very sight of it.

The reason why tanks resemble each other so closely is that every country is quick to spot an innovation by a rival nation – and copy it. This was especially true of suspension and tracks. The technical problems here were immense although the end products often look deceptively simple. Initially there were sets of bogies (sprung undercarriages with two pairs of wheels). From the bogie with two pairs of wheels there developed various combinations. There were numerous points to consider, such as whether the wheels should be all the same size, of small or large size, and, if varied, how positioned. Thus, some had large wheels at the end of the tracks and small ones in the middle, while others had large wheels in the middle and small ones at the ends. In practice certain tanks were found to have unexpected qualities such as being able to function when half the bogies had been shot away; others had a less satisfactory habit of breaking down from the most minor defects. In general large wheels were better for speed on level ground but small ones for uneven surfaces.

Basically tracks were simple enough, being chains around wheels. As a method of enabling vehicles to cross rough ground they had been in use for well over a

Theoretically, two men could operate a tank; in practice, at least five were necessary – and space was always at a premium.

hundred years when the tank was invented. One of the best designs of British tank had been submitted to the War Office in 1912. It was based on the experience which had already been gained from tracked vehicles. The inventor was an Australian named de Mole and his drawings of a tank – better in fact than any used later in the First World War – were put in the inevitable War Office pigeon-hole. It was said that somebody had scrawled across them 'This man must be mad.' De Mole visualized a flexible track which could be 'bowed' or bent thus conserving the power which other methods of steering lost. Track life tended to be short until manganese steel was used; even so, this left open the problem of best size and shape of track for rapid travel over hard ground or difficult progress over soft ground.

In view of the problems and potential weaknesses of tanks, as outlined above, it is hardly surprising that the PzKw I had many deficiencies when it was launched into war in Spain. Guderian stated that these tanks were only useful for training purposes and before being used in France or Eastern Europe should be considerably improved. Experience proved him right in that the armour was too thin and the armament too light. Nevertheless, 1445 PzKw Is were classed as operational in 1939; by 1941, 843 were still in use. The question immediately arises, 'Why if the Pzkw Is were so inadequate, were they so successful?' The answer is that they were successful because Allied tactics were so out of date. It may seem unbelievable that Britain which had pioneered the tank development should have remained so blind about operational strategy, but it was so.

The PzKw I had many qualities which fitted it for other uses than the forefront of battle. In 1939 it was envisaged as having a future as a reconnaissance link or as a light tank for use by airborne troops. A contract was placed with Krauss-Maffei AG in September 1939 for the development of forty tanks to be delivered in mid-1942. It would be a fast tank with a top speed of 40 mph. This model would have a weight of 8 tons and armour up to 30 mm thick. Three months later another contract for modification was placed, this time shared between Krauss-Maffei and Daimler-Benz. This time the tank was to be modified to make it into a battle tank with a weight of 18 tons and armour 80 mm thick. This version was to be armed with two MG34s but would, in view of its greater weight, have a top speed of only 16 mph. Other attempts to make use of obsolete PzKw components and production lines included experimental radio-controlled tanks, self-propelled guns (which were successful) and explosive charge layers. Some PzKw Is were used as command vehicles in 1939.

The PzKw II had a history almost as long as that of its elder brother but differed in certain essential details. A much more advanced type of tank had been designed – the PzKw III, to be followed by the PzKw IV, but these were delayed and a stopgap tank put into production. This, the PzKw II, was sometimes called the LKA–2 and was produced by Krupp, Henschel and Man. It was equipped with a 2 cm automatic cannon and a machine-gun. It had a maximum speed of 25 mph, weighed 7·2 tons and carried a crew of three. The suspension consisted of pairs of bogies attached to the hull by horizontal bars and leaf springs. Armour was 14·5 mm thick, and the Maybach 6 cylinder engine developed 140 hp. Various modifications were made in the years 1934–40 by which time the armour was 30 mm thick and the nose changed from round to square. There were nearly a thousand PzKw IIs available for service in France in 1940. A faster model was produced by Daimler-Benz in 1938, which used torsion-bar suspension, and was capable of 35 mph, but there were only 250 of them available by the end of 1939. They were known as *Schnellkampfwagen* (fast fighting vehicles). Other modifications to the basic model were made after the outbreak of war. The scope of the word 'modification' may be better understood when it is realized that a tank of the 1939 variety contained some 30,000 separate parts. Modification of any one of these would probably involve an alternative to adjoining components.

Early Panzers

The PzKw I, II and III were the first in the range of German medium tanks. The PzKw I (above) was in production as early as 1934 and was used in the Spanish Civil War; the PzKw II (left and above left) and III (below left) were produced or in production by 1940.

German tank resources received a tremendous boost when Czechoslovakia was overrun in the spring of 1939. The Czech Skoda factory had an international reputation in the armaments world and it was well justified. Not only did Germany gain 469 complete tanks, it also acquired the capacity to make many more. Until that moment the German Panzer force had been thinly equipped in relation to its needs. When Germany invaded Poland her total tank strength was 3195 and of these only 300 were of later design than PzKw I and PzKw II. Thus the Czech tanks were an enormous asset. Those who felt that the Munich Agreement of 1938, which enabled Hitler to swallow Czechoslovakia, was a diplomatic success were doubtless unaware that the presentation of Czech arms to Germany virtually assured its early victories. As an example, the 6th Panzer Division was equipped with LTM 35s (which became PzKw 35(t)s). This tank weighed just over 10 tons and was armed with a 37 mm gun and two machine-guns. The armour was 25 mm thick at the front and 16 mm along the sides. The engine gave it a speed of 25 mph and a range of over a hundred miles. It had other excellent qualities which gave the Panzers new ideas. The driving mechanism was at the rear, instead of at the front, and this meant more space in the centre of the tank. The engine, though powerful, was small. Suspension was more evenly balanced than was previously customary on the German models. Compressed air was used to assist transmission and steering, thus much reducing fatigue to the driver. These models proved extremely durable and when outmoded as tanks were still used as the chassis for military tractors and towing vehicles. Their only disadvantage was that they were constructed by riveting rather than welding. Another immensely valuable Czech tank was the TNHP–S, a product of Českomoravska Kolben Daněk of Prague, which became PzKw 38(t). In the Blitzkrieg of 1940 228 of these were used; the following year there were 763 of them in service. A year later they had been outclassed by the Russians, but the model continued to be modified up till 1945.

Soon after the beginning of the German campaign in Russia the Czechs were set to work to produce anti-tank weapons. As we have noted, a tank's vulnerability to attack depends largely on the thickness and toughness of its armour. Initially the Germans had not armoured their tanks very heavily, preferring the virtues of speed and mobility. It was assumed that the German air force would act as a mobile artillery unit and blast away intractable obstacles or anti-tank defences. On the Russian front, however, it became obvious that tanks must be made to destroy other tanks and this meant reinforcing them with

The Marder III: a product of the Russian 76·2 mm gun coupled to a Czech (38(t) chassis

Jägdpanzer IV, the tank hunter, equipped with anti-bazooka shields

more powerful guns. In order to counter Russian T34 tanks, captured Russian weapons were used. These 76·2 mm guns were mounted on the 38(t) chassis, and the superstructure was modified. These were known as Marder IIIs (Marder means marten). They were used extensively in 1943 and 1944.

Later versions of these Czech anti-tank tanks included the *Jagdpanzer* (tank hunter). This highly successful vehicle was used widely in 1944 and proved so effective that it was still produced after the end of the Second World War and sold to other armies, including the Swiss. Over 1500 were built in 1944. Its success derived from its very tough armour combined with exceptional mobility and effective firepower. Its weight was 16 tons. Another version, the *Flammenwerferpanzer* 38(t) had a flame-thrower in place of the 75 mm anti-tank gun.

There were a number of other variants of Czech tanks such as *Flakpanzer* (anti-aircraft tanks) and *Waffenträger*, but many of these belong to the later stages of the war. All through the war the Czech contribution to the Panzers – and other arms – was enormously valuable. However, at no time was it of greater value than in 1938–9. The Munich Agreement of 1938 has been given its place in history as an example of moral weakness, the betrayal of a brave but small democratic country to a bullying neighbour for 'peace at any price'. It was known that the Czechs had fifteen well-equipped divisions and the fact of handing over these to the potential enemy was noted at the time as being an act of military folly. What was not realized at the time, and is scarcely realized now, is that the Munich betrayal of the Czechs made it possible for Hitler to launch the Blitzkrieg of 1939 and 1940 and later made him able to continue the war on other fronts.

The invasion of Poland in 1939 was more of a gamble than it seemed at the time. In spite of the confident assertions of Guderian and the other tank pioneers the Panzers were still unproved. When Guderian led the Panzer force to Vienna in 1938 – to unite Austria to Germany by force – the Panzers had encountered more troubles than they cared to admit. At least thirty per cent had broken down en route and if this was the wastage rate in peacetime who could doubt that the wartime breakdowns against opposition and uneven surfaces would be at least twice as much? The figures from the occupation of Czechoslovakia were scarcely any better. Apart from the problems caused by mechanical breakdown and the fact that repairs could seldom be carried out on the spot it was obvious that the crews lacked experience. Furthermore, a single tank breaking down on a bridge or on a narrow road or being bogged down on a surface which had been destroyed by previous tanks could hold up an entire brigade. Fuel supplies, too, were a great problem. It was obvious that there was much more to the use of tanks than giving them good guns and strong armour. Mobile, mechanized warfare brought a series of problems which had never been envisaged.

Additionally, the experience of Spain was not one to encourage faith in the Panzer arm. Von Thoma was one of the great tank enthusiasts but his ardour had been notably dampened by his Spanish experience.

Nevertheless, there was a school of thought in the German army which believed that these were teething troubles and 'it would be all right on the day'. Only by war could a real test be made and in all probability the combination of Panzer and Luftwaffe would surprise the world. In the event it did but only because of the short-sightedness of their opponents.

Fortunately for Germany there was in 1939 a potential opponent with just the right equipment on exactly the right terrain. Nobody, not even in Germany, had believed the rantings of Hitler that Germans were being oppressed in Austria, Czechoslovakia or Poland but the opportunity to invade and right their imaginary wrongs with the excellent chance of a swift victory was an exciting prospect. To the creators of the Panzer force it was almost too good to be true. If the Panzers were as good as they were thought to be they would make mincemeat of the opposition which consisted of thirty ill-equipped infantry divisions and eleven cavalry brigades. The cavalry brigades were genuine cavalry, with horses, not the armoured units which cavalry has subsequently become. The Poles had but one armoured unit, a single brigade. Against this the Germans could muster seven Panzer divisions, four motorized infantry divisions, four light divisions, and forty orthodox infantry divisions. The spearhead was of course the Panzers with their concentration of tanks. Apart from the tanks in the armoured brigade the Poles spread their tanks (they had 660 at the start of the campaign) throughout their army.

The campaign gave a swift foretaste of what the world might expect from Nazi Germany. It was preceded by a blast of propaganda which was meant to persuade Britain, who had guaranteed Polish independence, that her intervention in this domestic matter would be quite unjustified. The propaganda was ineffective but Britain had no chance whatever of helping Poland. There were various theories of 'armchair strategy' current at the time and their inanity may be shown by quoting one. It was believed that the RAF could fly over Germany, bomb at will, and land in Poland for refuelling, spares and rearming. This fearful prospect, it was assumed, would deter the Germans. Unfortunately, there were a few problems such as range of aircraft, standardization of equipment, navigation and spares which had been overlooked. But thousands of people genuinely believed this hypothesis.

In the event the Poles had no one to rely on but themselves. If Britain and France had promptly made an attempt to invade western Germany, history might have been different. Neither country was in a position to do so. The Germans, on the other hand, had temporarily disposed of the problem of Russian interference by the Molotov-Ribbentrop Pact. Germany invaded Poland without warning, when the latter was still mobilizing. Further surprise was added by the use of dive-bombers which, screaming down from the sky, have an effect on the morale of inexperienced troops which is well beyond the physical damage they inflict. But the Poles were not easy victims, even though the campaign lasted a mere nineteen days. At one point they charged tanks with horsed cavalry – and the result was to damage some of the tanks. This was the spirit which the Poles would show later in the war.

Poles Make Defence Move Along 945-Mile Front

GERMAN HIGH COMMAND CLAIMS FALL OF WARSAW

A COMMUNIQUE broadcast by the German High Command last night announced that German motorised troops entered Warsaw at 5.15 p.m.

There is no confirmation of this claim, and reports from Warsaw state the Polish Army is still intact and that forces have withdrawn to their pre-established defence positions along a 945-mile front.

The Lord Mayor of Warsaw, M. Starzynski, was heard speaking on the Warsaw radio at 7.15 p.m. He asked the people of the city to dig trenches and to prepare for the defence of the capital.

Another German report says that troops were advancing on Warsaw from three directions and were within 25 miles of the capital, the "fall of which is inevitable."

Crowded hospital trains have been arriving at the Potsdamer station, Berlin, with wounded soldiers from the front.

(Messages from Reuter, Associated Press and Exchange).

Cautious reporting of the first major German victory of the war

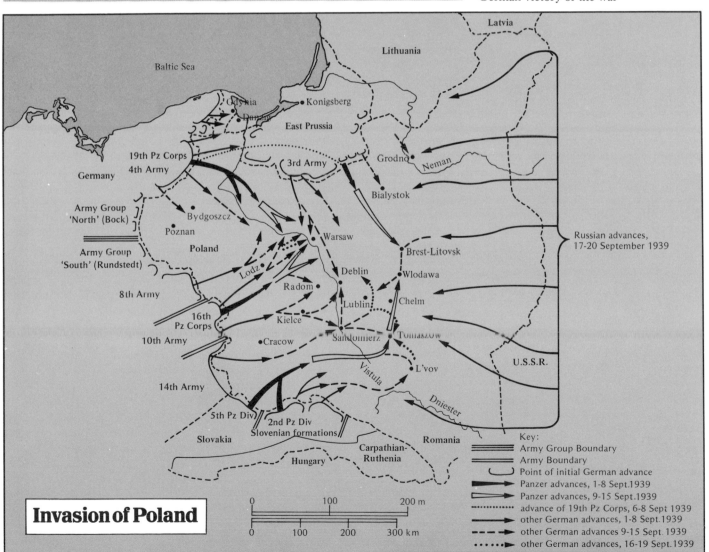

Invasion of Poland

For the moment it was a matter of men against machines, of flesh against metal. The Poles had 225 tanks, most of them obsolete, and 360 aircraft. The Luftwaffe had 1250 operational aircraft. The entire Polish air force was destroyed within the first two days.

Apart from dispersing their tanks too widely, the Poles made another fundamental mistake in trying to guard the whole of their eight-hundred-mile-long frontier. This was fatal against the Panzers for the speed which this new weapon brought to warfare meant that once a breakthrough had been achieved penetration could be so deep that there was no point in the Poles trying to hold the intact part of the frontier. If they did so the units in that position would be isolated as the Germans fanned out into the rear areas. It was not necessary for the Germans to destroy many Polish strongpoints; they could bypass them. The fact that dive-bombers hurtled down from the sky in remote areas all helped to reinforce the assault on Polish morale. The confusion caused by deep Panzer thrusts, and the bombing of undefended towns sent a host of refugees on to the roads. This was all part of Panzer theory. Anything which blocked the roads and prevented the enemy using reinforcements was justified. Refugees on crowded roads were machine-gunned from the air, not because the casualties were important but because this action led to further civilian panic and even greater obstruction. Busily at work, too, were many of the two million German residents in Poland. These, if not actively practising physical sabotage, would be spreading rumours of the successes of the Germans, the alleged trickery and cowardice of the Polish leaders and the inevitability of German victory. This last policy was known as *Schrecklichkeit*, which may be translated as 'frightfulness'. Britain and France were inclined to discount these reports when they arrived, thinking them to be the fevered imaginings of people reeling under the shock of defeat, but when France was invaded the following summer the stories were found to have been all too true.

German strategy in Poland was to attack with three deep pincer movements with subsidiary movements fanning outwards from the main claws. The innermost pincer skirted around Bydgoszez with its northern claw and Lodz with the southern. Both closed in towards Warsaw. The middle claw in the north was made up of the 3rd Army which was conveniently stationed due north of Warsaw in East Prussia. (East Prussia was a piece of German territory separated from Germany by a neck of Polish territory known as the Polish Corridor. This unfortunate situation dated from the re-establishment of the Polish nation after the First World War.) The German 3rd Army sent one prong directly to Warsaw, and another one towards Brest Litovsk. Of the southern claws one curved upwards past Radom to Warsaw and another headed towards Brest-Litovsk via Chelm. A smaller prong from this arm drove towards Lodz.

That was the simple strategy of the Polish campaign. Nothing like it had been known before. There were mistakes, of course, for tanks ran out of fuel and roads became blocked, but overall it was a devastating success. It was not quite as bloodless for the Germans as it was thought to be. The Germans lost 10,572 killed in action and another 5,029 missing. 'Missing' usually means killed but may mean taken prisoner. The Poles were hardly in a position to take prisoners. There were 30,322 German wounded. For this price the Germans conquered a nation of 33 million people. As the Russians intervened to 'help', Germany lost 13 million and most of the oil she badly wanted. But this was no time to confront the Russians.

The southern prongs were launched by Army Group South which was commanded by General Karl von Rundstedt. His Chief of Staff was General Erich von Manstein. Army Group North was commanded by General Feodor von Bock. Guderian was in the northern sector leading 19th Corps. By being in the forefront of the battle with his command tank he was able to prove his theories about the commander needing to be at a point where he can see for himself the progress of the battle and make decisions without the normal delay. This is good common sense, for it is obvious that if important decisions are made

only when information has been passed back to a rear HQ, and then the decision has to be transmitted forward and given to the addressee who may well be on the move, much time is lost. However, the exposure of important commanders to the everyday hazard of front-line war is likely to be a waste of scarce resources. Guderian himself was caught by fire from his own supporting artillery which was somewhat rashly firing into the mist. He was lucky to escape. Major-General von Mellenthin quotes an example of another German general who had a narrow escape when visiting a forward unit. A low-flying aircraft circled over corps headquarters looking for a landing ground. Although the plane

PREVIOUS PAGES A PzKw II parade through the streets of Warsaw

BELOW During the invasion of Poland the Panzers discovered that even rivers were no obstacle to their progress.

was German and carried German markings, this did not stop a number of soldiers firing at it. According to von Mellenthin, 'Soon afterwards the aircraft landed and out stepped the Luftwaffe general responsible for our close air support. He failed to appreciate the joke.'

Under the fast-moving conditions of Panzer warfare troops are liable to shoot first and think second. This can produce unfortunate results and examples were given of Germans firing on other Germans, either because they did not recognize their uniforms or simply because they did not expect to encounter German troops in that place. The Germans learned many lessons, at all levels. Lessons learned in one campaign do not necessarily apply to another, at command level, but the experience of being under fire and winning victories is an enormous boost for morale and general steadiness in the fighting troops.

The lesson which should have been learned by Germany's future opponents, but appears to have been unheeded, was that the Panzers did not always choose 'good tank country'. Instead they sometimes went through heavily wooded country or over hills. Eight months later the Allies were surprised when the Panzers attacked France through the Ardennes, for the Ardennes country was considered to be 'unsuitable for tanks'.

Von Thoma, commanding a brigade in the southern sector, had a happier experience than he had known in Spain.

Not least of the factors contributing to Panzer success was the presence of close-support military aircraft. With these the obsolete Polish air force was destroyed, mainly on the ground, before it could do any damage. The Luftwaffe was then free to harass the civilian population, to assist the Panzers and to fly reconnaissance missions.

The Germans did not have matters all their own way, as the casualty figures show. One example occurred to the west of Warsaw where the German 10th Army was running short of fuel and the 8th Army was at the end of a long thrust. There the Poles counter-attacked and from 9 to 15 September held the Germans and even drove them back. Eventually the Poles were defeated by the rapidity with which the Germans were able to concentrate aircraft and tanks to meet this new threat. The Poles had hoped, but hoped in vain, that the French were about to invade western Germany, where the defences had been stripped to the minimum and there were no Panzers. Had the French done so they could have achieved considerable success, for there was so little to oppose them. The French had apparently promised an invasion on 17 September but by that time all was virtually over in Poland.

Another lesson of the Polish war was that rivers were not as important an obstacle to tanks as had been feared. Although none of this generation of tanks was amphibious, the mobile bridging sections could be brought up so rapidly that there was little delay. Had the Poles been able to mass adequate artillery on the other bank it might have been a different story. The General Staff was encouraged to find that the percentage of mechanical breakdowns was less than on the earlier forays, twenty-five instead of thirty per cent. Even so, twenty-five per cent is a quarter of the total force. There had been 217 tanks knocked out but if the war had not ended quickly many more tanks would have become unusable pending major servicing. The PzKw Is and IIs had acquitted themselves well in the circumstances; the opposition was not well-armed but the mileage task was gruelling. Guderian's corps achieved two hundred miles in ten days, which in view of the fact that it ran into some stiff opposition is a remarkable performance.

Overall the speed and mobility of the Panzers had been almost everything the German army had asked for. Less satisfactory was the failure of the motorized infantry to keep up. These were carried in trucks which are aptly known as 'soft-skinned vehicles'. Their reluctance to expose themselves to almost certain destruction, for they were obvious targets, caused large gaps to open up between themselves and the spearheads. Marching divisions had also been left well behind; horsed cavalry had hardly come into the picture at all.

3 Blitzkrieg, 1940

The lesson of the Polish campaign had little effect on Allied strategy. In so far as Germany's other opponents were concerned, the general impression was that the Polish campaign bore little resemblance to what they themselves might have to expect. Poland's failure to stop the Germans was attributed to poor organization and outdated equipment. Both, of course, were contributory factors but in underestimating the contribution of the new Panzer units the Allies were making a dangerous miscalculation.

Strangely enough, the view of the German General Staff was not dissimilar to that of the Allies. Here, too, was the feeling that the luck and success of Poland could not be repeated against the French and British. There was a marked respect for the Anglo-French armies which were now in position in France; this was hardly surprising in view of the fact that Germany had suffered defeat by them a mere twenty-five years before. It was widely known that the Panzers had run into serious trouble in the Warsaw suburbs, in fact 57 out of 120 tanks had been destroyed in a single day. The German General Staff visualized the consequences of that happening in Northern France. The problem with Panzers was that in order to function at all they had to be self-contained, balanced units. Because they were fast-moving and ranged across the countryside, they needed to take their own ancillary units and service echelon with them. They needed their own reconnaissance units, perhaps armoured cars, perhaps motor cyclists, perhaps infantrymen (in certain areas). They needed a brigade of infantry in each division and if that brigade was to be moved rapidly

PREVIOUS PAGES The invasion of France: a PzKw III column at Aisne, 1940

BELOW Rivers were not insurmountable obstacles to the Panzers, even though they were not amphibious. It was expedient for an engineering crew to travel with the units to construct bridges like this one.

it needed armoured personnel carriers (APCs) with half tracks to enable them to move where there were no roads. The infantry would include such varied elements as rifle platoons, machine-gunners, mortar-teams, and anti-tank units. Sometimes they even included howitzers for dealing with obstacles beyond the range of mortars.

Artillery was essential, partly for providing covering fire (including smoke). This meant large calibre weapons such as 75 mm guns and 105 mm howitzers. In the early stages these were towed but later were mainly self-propelled. One part of the artillery was allotted to anti-tank duties and another to anti-aircraft fire. The Germans used their 88 mm gun for both purposes. It was a formidable all-round weapon which was heartily disliked by those who confronted it. Curiously enough, the British 3·7 in anti-aircraft gun was a better weapon but was never used in an anti-tank role. This seems to have been one of the most extraordinary anomalies of the war.

Engineers were needed, not merely for bridging and demolitions, but for laying or clearing mines. Signals were, of course, the life-blood of the unit.

No other formation relied so heavily on its service element as did the Panzers. Fuel, ammunition and food had to be brought up whatever the circumstances and difficulties. Spares, and repair and maintenance were equally vital, as were of course medical units for attending to and removing casualties. It is the custom in all armies to begrudge the size of the service element, which is often spoken of in disparaging terms, but without it a Panzer division – and others – would quickly come to a halt. Nevertheless, the service 'tail' of a Panzer division tended to clutter up roads. In 1940 air supply was in its infancy and the helicopter a dream of the future.

To ensure that all their demands were fulfilled the Panzers needed a sympathetic and energetic supporter at top level on the supply side. This they failed to get as General Friedrich Fromm, who was ultimately responsible for their needs, was distinctly lukewarm to the whole Panzer concept.

The German army which stood ready to be launched in the May 1940 Blitzkrieg had many advantages over its future opponents. It still had the same

The Czech PzKw 35(t) tank which, with the 38(t), replaced the PzKw Is.

The Czech 38(t) tank

number of tanks as before, a total of 3379, of which 2574 were front line. The French had a similar number of tanks in their forward units but with the fatal difference that theirs were widely dispersed whereas the Panzers were concentrated on a narrow front (less than a hundred miles). The British had 310 tanks with another 300 on the way; the quality was good but the quantity speaks for itself. The German tanks had the benefit of having to prove themselves in Poland and this meant that some had been uparmoured. A number of PzKw Is had been replaced by Czech PzKw 35(t) and 38(t) tanks.

The initial German invasion plan bore a close resemblance to that of 1914, the famous Schlieffen Plan. This had been designed to swing in a great arc, violating Belgian neutrality on the way, and to encircle Paris in a hook movement. The 'hook' concept fascinated German strategists and became a feature of armoured warfare wherever it was possible. By 1940 the Panzer generals realized that a successful 'hook' meant much more than simply breaking the front line. It could also involve fighting onwards through solid obstructions.

Hitler had originally planned the attack in the west for November 1939. After the Polish victory he had offered peace to the western nations. He can hardly have thought his proposals would be heeded, but propaganda and treachery had been his constant companions for so long that he may have imagined they could continue to be successful forever. On receiving the curt rejection in October 1939 he ordered plans to be made for the western campaign. In spite of the Molotov-Ribbentrop Pact, which had freed his hands for the Polish invasion, he felt that the Russians were merely biding their time. In November 1939 Russia swallowed Finland, possibly through fear of Germany. Russia's move into Finland confirmed the German belief that Russia was on the march and in due course would reach Germany. But a November blitzkrieg into France was prevented by weather which grounded the German air force. This apparent setback was in fact an incalculable benefit, for it caused a change in the whole German strategy.

The German plan for invasion in November 1939 would have used all ten Panzer divisions in Belgium coming in by each side of Liège. This was Army Group B. Army Group C was to come up and confront the Maginot Line but not to attack it. Army Group A, in which von Manstein was Chief of Staff, was to come in through the Ardennes with infantry, and advance to the Meuse. Von Manstein felt it was all too like 1914 and spoke his mind. He preferred an attack in which only three Panzer divisions would be used in Belgium and Holland but would be supported by all the airborne units, thus creating the impression this was the main thrust. Seven Panzers would simultaneously be launched through the Ardennes, to cross the Meuse at Sedan and to come in behind the Allied troops who by this time would presumably all be rushing up into Belgium. The Ardennes sector would be difficult for tanks but the Polish experience had established that tanks could manage 'unsuitable' tank country. The Allies, of course, did not appreciate the fact that the Panzers could cope with Ardennes-type terrain and would not visualize a tank threat in this area.

Von Manstein's plan received qualified support. It was daring, imaginative and original. It would certainly surprise the opposition if it worked. But there were some who felt it might not work.

The decision to use it depended on a curious incident in January 1940. A German aircraft carrying the original plan went off course and landed in Belgium. Nobody in Germany knew whether the plan had been destroyed or not. Certainly the risk of using it now would be too great. In consequence, von Manstein's plan was adopted.

At 05.30 on the fatal 10 May 1940 Germany launched her attack on the west. Germany had air superiority but on the ground was inferior both in numbers of divisions and numbers of tanks. In overall quality there was little to choose between the opposing tanks, but there was a vital difference in that the Germans had concentrated theirs in armoured divisions whereas the Allies spaced theirs out among the infantry. This was an important reason for subsequent German success but not the only one. Other reasons included the endless preparation and rehearsal which had been practised in Germany, on the Mosel and elsewhere, during the winter months. It is a military axiom that if a certain manoeuvre has been practised often enough in peacetime it will be carried through with much the same precision even when there is opposition. The need to conserve fuel and ammunition precluded the ability to practise certain manoeuvres but others were brought to perfection. Thus, in the north, Army Group B hurled itself over the frontiers, preceded by devastating waves of Stuka bombers. The fact that this was not the main attack did not make it any less formidable. The French were using their tanks which were frequently better armed than the Panzers but this availed them little, for the Panzers were handled so much more adroitly. When a German Panzer met a French Somua the Panzer would exchange shots then veer away, either to slip past the Frenchman or to wait until another Panzer came up to join in. The French tanks, taught to form a line in front of the Infantry, were at a loss when attacked from the flanks and behind. Courage, of which they had plenty, availed little in this unnatural twisting battle line. The Germans did not wish to make too much progress in this area for if the Allies fell back too far the remainder of the Manstein Plan could be affected. The French had four armoured divisions but these bore little resemblance to the ideal. All had been created hastily since the fall of Poland, and all were equipped with short-range Char B tanks. The Char B had a 75 mm gun and 60 mm of armour-plate, but its weakness lay in the fact that the commander was the gunner and the 75 mm could only be traversed by slewing around the tank. The armoured divisions were known by the abbreviation DCR (*Division Cuirassée*), whereas the cavalry divisions, intended mainly for

Snow effectively prohibited the Panzer advance to Moscow.

In view of the innumerable hazards and obstacles which beset the Panzers on their drive across Russia, it is understandable that the order to halt Barbarossa temporarily was considered highly ironic.

At dawn, 10 May 1940, German armoured divisions mass for the invasion of the West.

reconnaissance, were named the DLMs (*Division Légère Mécanique*). Unfortunately the DCRs, although equipped with tanks of great potential, were undertrained. It was reported that some of the personnel, signals and artillery included, had never practised with their units until they joined them to fight the Panzers. North of Dinant the 1st DCR was given the task of stopping Rommel's 7th Panzer Division. Before they could come to blows the DCR ran out of petrol. Rommel took the crews prisoner and having refuelled the tanks took them with his own to use as reinforcements, using the French drivers for the time being. A brave attempt was made by the 2nd and 3rd DCR to check Guderian's 19th and 41st Corps. A corps usually contains two or more divisions, so that the French were hopelessly outnumbered. They had, in fact, a good opportunity to hit Guderian on the flank but shortage of fuel and command muddle frittered away the chance. General Charles de Gaulle, who had long passionately

advocated the establishment of a strong, well-trained French armoured force, commanded 4th DCR. His enthusiasm was ultimately rewarded with the command of a division lacking in most of its artillery and infantry. It made an attempt against Guderian at Montcornet but was easily brushed aside. The humiliation of this experience left an indelible mark on the General's character.

A German tank being transported across the Meuse after breaking through the Ardennes

Finding a way through the Ardennes proved less arduous than expected. The Germans had made very careful preparations. Every yard of the ground had been carefully mapped, every French strongpoint was known. Immediately prior to the invasion there had been a large influx of sturdy looking civilian 'tourists'. As the Panzers approached, the 'tourists' busied themselves by demolishing road blocks, removing charges from bridges and spreading rumours of imminent and terrible disaster among an apprehensive population. The fact that the French were unable to blow up bridges when they wished to had an exceptionally alarming effect. The nervous were encouraged to leave their homes and in looking for safety to block those very roads along which the French defence wished to travel. Meanwhile, all was going reasonably smoothly with the Panzers although elements from one division did occasionally tangle with another as they pressed forward. Dinant was the target of the 15th, Monthermé of the 41st Corps and Sedan of the 19th Corps. They reached the Meuse on the morning of 13 May and, with massive air cover, launched their infantry across. Two were across by afternoon and were building bridges for their tanks. It was a critical stage for a fierce French attack by the 9th Army, with air support, could have swept the flimsy bridgeheads back into the river. Unfortunately, the commander of the 9th Army made the incorrect assessment that the Germans were too strongly entrenched and decided to withdraw. This would not in itself have been a disastrous decision if an attempt had been made to cut off the Panzer troops which were now ranging far and wide with reckless abandon. By the fifteenth all were across the Meuse and Rommel's 7th Panzer Division

ABOVE Despite the hopelessness of their situation and without hope of any auxiliary support the Panzers pushed on to Moscow.

RIGHT After the frost and the thaw yet another natural obstacle immobilized the Panzers: dust.

OPPOSITE After the invasion of France Germany transported Panzers to N. Africa to open another front.

was past Philippeville. The French High Command seemed to be paralysed, so much so that General Maurice Gamelin himself (on the nineteenth) decided to take charge of the battle. It was too late. At the moment of decision he was replaced by the ageing General Maxime Weygand, hero of the First World War, but now set an almost impossible task. The Panzers were now moving forward at an average speed of nineteen miles a day; on one day (20 May) Guderian's 19th Corps managed fifty-six miles. On the way they overran astonished French army posts and set another army of refugees on the march. When the opposition became formidable – as occasionally it did – they closed up and hammered the obstruction with their artillery while the Stukas joined in the general destruction. Their greatest handicap was the slowness of the infantry, which periodically had to be allowed to catch up. Where it could the French army made a dogged stand, although morale was beginning to be affected.

With the Panzers now deep into France, the German High Command had to decide whether it would be better to strike for Paris or to race to the coast and establish a salient across the line of communication of the armies fighting in Belgium. Either way the Allied command was tangled in knots. The Panzer supply services were working much better than anticipated and captured French depots made a useful contribution. Periodically tanks needed to stop for maintenance but it was clear that they could continue the battle for several days longer. It was against all precedent and reason but it was happening. Even the vaunted Maginot Line proved an overrated obstacle. Rommel had more luck than he deserved – as successful commanders tend to. The infantry of his spearhead, the 25th Panzer, ran into a British regiment of Matilda tanks whose guns contemptuously shrugged off the German 37 mm anti-tank gun-fire. The arrival of an artillery regiment of 88 mm guns made life rather less satisfactory for the British but as the tanks of the 25th Panzer came back to save their infantry – too

Transporting the infantry was extremely time-consuming and presented the major obstacle to Panzer efficiency. In the foreground is a self-propelled gun, followed by armoured personnel carriers on the road to Paris in 1940.

Nothing stood in the way of the Panzers

OVERLEAF In a French coastal town, a scene of devastation: the inevitable signpost of the path of the Panzers

late, they were caught by the British 2-pounders, a very effective weapon, and lost twenty tanks. It was said that this mauling of an impetuous Panzer regiment convinced Hitler that the British were merely biding their time and that if the Panzers pressed forward too recklessly they were unlikely ever to see Germany again.

Hitler's doubts about the wisdom of their continuing deep thrusts was shared by many in the High Command. It seemed impossible that the French and British defence could be torn apart so easily and that the Manstein Plan could be working so smoothly. No such doubts assailed the Panzer commanders; they had supreme confidence in their weapons and their methods.

The psychology of the Panzers, whether senior officers or crew, was not new, but had not been seen on battlefields for many years. Destruction in the First World War and in the wars which preceded it had been enormous but at least it had principally involved the destruction of other soldiers. The Panzers, however, were ravaging France in much the same way as the Huns and Tartars had ravaged countries in ancient times. The route of the Panzers was marked by burning villages and by the indiscriminate slaughter of civilians, including women and children, who simply happened to be on the Panzer route. There was no time to distinguish between military and other targets, nor does it seem that it was policy to do so. Enclosed in his tank the Panzer trooper felt himself apart from the normal world; the sight of burning buildings, mutilated bodies, the smell of burning flesh made less impact on him in his insulated cocoon than it might have done had he been on foot. Ruthlessness was an essential characteristic of Panzer warfare; in the years to come many of the crews which had rampaged jubilantly and remorselessly through France would taste the bitterness of defeat in their turn. With a tank the transition from triumph to disaster can be so swift as to be almost incomprehensible. At one moment the tank is surging forward, blasting obstacles out of the way or crushing them beneath its

LEFT Rommel directed his Panzer forces brilliantly even when they were severely reduced in number.

ABOVE German Panzers opposing Mark 1V light tanks of the British regiment during the siege of Tobruk, 1941; painting by Wilhelm Wessel.

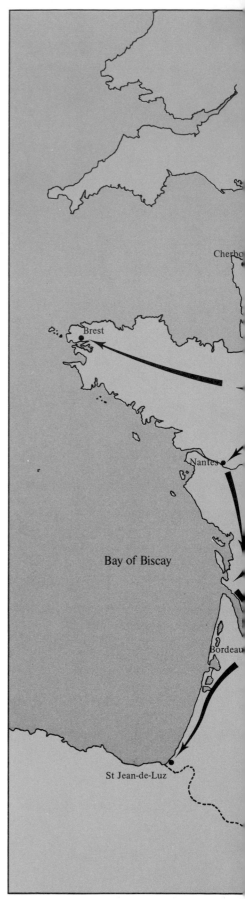

tracks; in the next it is helpless, either useless and pathetic or a blazing death-trap from which its crew vainly try to escape. But in France in 1940 the nemesis of the Panzers seemed far away; they drove to their targets with the ruthless determination which had been stamped on the corps by those leaders who, fresh from the destruction and misery of the First World War, could see nothing better than to lay the foundations of even greater destruction in the Second World War.

Progress across France encountered few checks, and what there were came partly from the German High Command. Guderian pushed on fifty-five miles beyond Sedan and was halted by von Rundstedt who said he must venture no farther. Guderian bypassed the order by requesting permission for 'reconnaissance'. On the seventeenth the Panzers were across the Oise, and on the eighteenth at St Quentin. From St Quentin they began racing across the Somme, on the twentieth they reached Abbeville. On the twenty-first they halted. At Arras that day the 15th Panzer Corps was in trouble when it was attacked by an Allied force, but the 19th Panzer Corps was able to start up the Atlantic Coast on the twenty-second and head for Boulogne. Some of the Panzer thrusts were then receiving the attention of the Luftwaffe who, seeing moving columns, could not at first believe they were Germans – and bombed them. Guderian reached Boulogne which was garrisoned by the British 20th Guards Brigade. Medievalists will be interested to note that the presence of the indomitable British Guards was not his only problem; the ancient city walls were just as intractable and took a very heavy battering before they were breached. The ability of ancient fortifications to withstand the pounding of modern weapons from land and air is a phenomenon which never fails to surprise military commanders. Calais fell on the twenty-sixth after a formidable resistance in which one British brigade held up three German divisions. It seemed as if all was over for the Allies and that Hitler's dream of establishing an empire which would last for a thousand years was well on its way to being realized. Nevertheless, all was not lost. Weygand was making an admirable attempt to fight back in the Somme area. The fact that the Allied forces had been sliced through by the

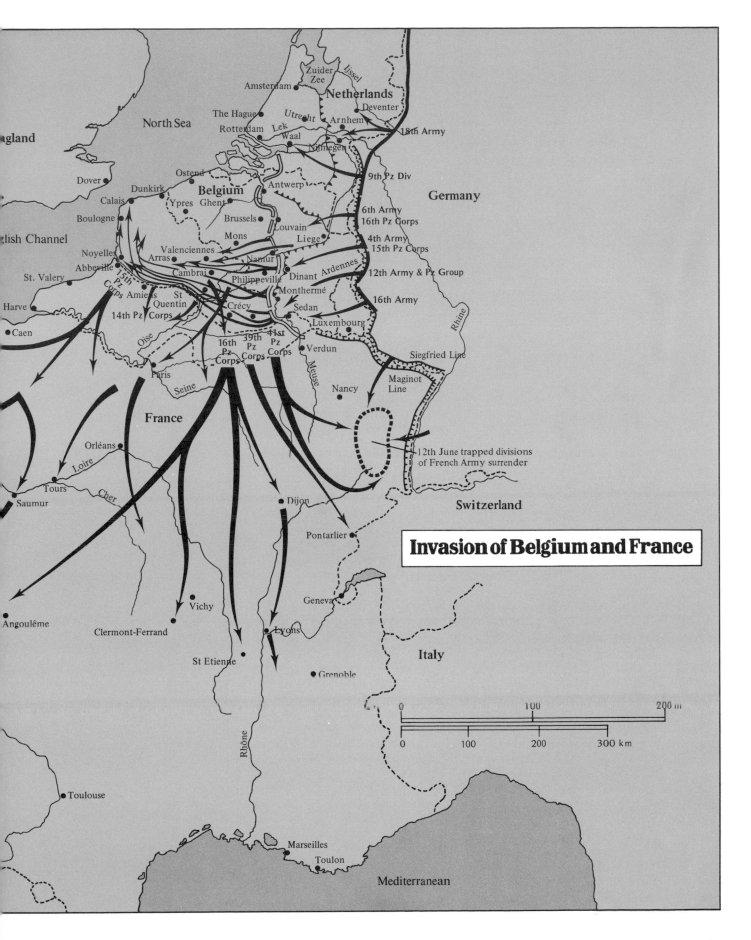

Zuider Zee
IJssel
Amsterdam
Netherlands
Deventer
The Hague
Utrecht
Arnhem
Rotterdam
Lek
18th Army
Waal
Nijmegen
North Sea
9th Pz Div
Ostend
Dover
Antwerp
Germany
Dunkirk
Belgium
6th Army
Calais
Ypres
Ghent
16th Pz Corps
Boulogne
Brussels
Louvain
4th Army
lish Channel
Mons
Liege
15th Pz Corps
Noyelles
Valenciennes
Namur
Arras
St. Valery
Abbeville
Cambrai
Dinant
Ardennes
12th Army & Pz Group
15th Pz Corps
Philippeville
Harve
Amiens
St
Montthermé
16th Army
Caen
14th Pz Corps
Quentin
Crécy
Sedan
Oise
16th
39th
41st
Luxembourg
Pz
Pz
Pz
Verdun
Siegfried Line
Paris
Corps
Corps
Corps
Meuse
Seine
Nancy
Maginot
Line
France
Orléans
12th June trapped divisions
of French Army surrender
Loire
Tours
Cher
Saumur
Dijon
Switzerland
Pontarlier
Invasion of Belgium and France
Angoulême
Vichy
Geneva
Clermont-Ferrand
Lyons
Italy
St Etienne
Grenoble
100
200 m
Rhône
0
100
200
300 km
Toulouse
Marseilles
Toulon
Mediterranean

OPPOSITE Panzers begin the second phase
of the invasion of Russia.

ABOVE A knocked-out camouflaged
Russian T34 tank; two survivors are
taken prisoner.

Panzers was a disaster but it did not necessarily mean the end of the campaign. There were still men with arms on the Allied side. If resistance could be rallied and organized the forebodings of the German GHQ about the recklessness of the Panzer thrusts could well be proved right. The 51st Highland Division fought a dogged retreating battle to St Valery-en-Caux, where what was left of it finally surrendered on 12 June. There is a memorial to them on the hill above the town. There is another form of memorial at St Valery in the shape of the massive German defences, the West Wall, which were built during the occupation – but built in vain.

Mussolini declared war on France on 10 June, which his friends as well as his foes thought showed a sense of timing well in tune with his character. Fighting in France was not quite over; one of the more gallant examples was the action by the staff and students of Saumur Cavalry Academy. De Gaulle, too, kept on doggedly to the last. Henri Pétain had ordered the French army to cease fighting on 17 June but many chose to ignore him and went on fighting till the twenty-fifth.

The most astonishing decision of the war was the German reluctance to drive the Panzers into Dunkirk where the remnants of the British and French armies had finally congregated. The German High Command, already nervous about the way the Panzers were roaming through the countryside, feared they must

OPPOSITE Guderian, who promoted the idea of tank warfare in the 1920s, held a command post during the Western offensive and was responsible for emphasizing the importance of adequate radio communications, particularly between the tank units.

BELOW Brauchitsch (left) and Kluge (right) near Paris in June 1940

Victorious Panzers approaching the Arc de Triomphe; Paris is theirs.

have outstripped their supplies and be literally at the end of their tether; in consequence they ordered a halt. It was said that the order came directly from Hitler, but the record shows that he endorsed it but did not initiate it. It was felt that the Allied evacuation could be prevented by the Luftwaffe and to push exhausted Panzers into Dunkirk, which would presumably be bristling with anti-tank guns and desperate men, would be folly of the highest order. In fact the men were utterly exhausted and in some cases had lost their weapons. The 'trap' which the Germans feared simply did not exist.

By the time the Panzers began moving again the great opportunity had been lost. In the nine days of the 'miracle of Dunkirk' 338,226 Allied soldiers, of which 120,000 were French, were rescued. Vast quantities of equipment were left behind; these could be replaced but men could not. Many more could have been rescued, from Boulogne and Calais, but it was considered that if they had been taken off the Allies would have felt that the British were predominantly looking after their own nationals.

The war in France was not quite over. The Panzers were still hungrily looking for fresh conquests. Part of the 15th Corps had reached Cherbourg on 19 June but not without being punished by the French artillery. Although the British Expeditionary Force and the French troops from Belgium had been evacuated, the rest of the French army was making the Panzers pay a price for victory. Paris had been abandoned on 13 June and occupied by German infantry. The rest of the 15th Corps drove on to Brest which they also reached on 19 June.

In the middle of France was a different story. Contrary to general belief, all resistance in France had not crumbled on the evacuation of Dunkirk. In the Amiens-Peronne area the 14th and 16th Panzer groups had had a rough handling from French tanks and artillery and not until Guderian's 34th and 41st Panzer Groups crossed the Aisne, to drive south, did the other two groups begin to push down into the central sector.

Guderian reached the Swiss frontier on the sixteenth, thereby encircling the French forces in that area. The other Panzers reached Angoulême, Clermont-Ferrand and St Etienne by 25 June.

The Panzers had succeeded beyond their most optimistic expectations. There was no doubt in anyone's mind that the swift and devastating victory had been largely due to the Panzers. The Luftwaffe had certainly played a vital role, and apart from material destruction had spread terror and confusion on an enormous scale. 'Frightfulness' had been an integral part of the campaign but the main legacy of hate was against the Luftwaffe and the sinister SS, not against the Panzers. Losses in terms of German lives had been low; losses in material had been higher than expected. Although the German tanks had done all and more than had been expected of them, serious deficiencies had been revealed. The light tanks were not fast enough; the larger ones were not quite sturdy enough to deal with all opposition. British and French heavy tanks had proved too good for the PzKw IVs and had there been more of them in the right places at the right time the Panzer attack would have been blunted. A serious German deficiency had been the lack of adequate armoured personnel carriers to bring up the infantry.

Overall the Panzers had proved their point conclusively. Sceptics who had dismissed the Polish successes as victories over negligible opposition now had to eat their words. The Panzers had destroyed a large Allied force by dash, speed and determination. Whatever strategic and tactical mistakes had been made had not been made by the Panzers. Henceforth their prestige was un-challengeable. Hitler, of course, was delighted with them and decreed that their numbers should be increased. The obvious power of the Panzers gave a new dimension to his plans which, in the future, would be related to Panzer capacity and limitations. A first step would be to double the existing stocks of armoured vehicles. The fact that Germany, even after her new conquests, had not the resources to undertake such a task made no difference to Hitler's grandiose plans. This is the weakness of a dictatorship. Authoritarianism gets work done but the leader is usually so powerful that no one dares tell him that some of his ideas are nonsensical. Hitler's orders were obeyed. The number of Panzer divisions was doubled. What no one could tell Hitler was that the total stock of armoured vehicles remained roughly the same, even including the captured vehicles, and the armoured personnel carriers which had been shown to be such a vital need in France simply could not be produced in the required quantity. There was another unknown factor. Could the new Panzers, diluted with newcomers, maintain the standards of the originals? Time alone would tell.

4 Operation Barbarossa

The successes of the Panzers, which gave Hitler the confidence to invade Russia, had not been confined to Poland and France. In the latter campaign most of the credit went to the Panzers which had driven in through the Ardennes but it should not be overlooked that those assigned the task of overrunning Holland and Belgium, before heading in the direction of Arras, played a vital part, too.

The Panzers were given another task in 1941. This was to take part in the conquest of the Balkans. The campaign produced a series of easy victories but in the opinion of the Panzer leaders gave them little valuable experience to compensate for the wastage of tanks. When Hitler said that Panzer strength would be doubled, bringing it up to twenty-one divisions, this had meant that tank strength was cut by half. In future each regiment would have less than 200 tanks. As the strength of the Panzers had partly depended on their being able to concentrate large groups of tanks rapidly, and 'smother' a target, any dilution of tank strength was clearly going to affect tactics and overall performance. Nevertheless, the Balkan campaign employed Panzers and lost some in the process.

The object of the Balkan campaign was to occupy Greece and thus deny the Allies the use of the airfields. Germany was relying heavily on Romanian oil and any threat to this supply had to be dealt with promptly. That threat existed as long as British aircraft might fly from Greek bases and bomb the oilfields.

The capture of Greece meant a campaign in Yugoslavia as well, and this was duly launched on 6 April 1941. It was concluded eleven days later, but not without cost. Yugoslavia did not possess a single tank nor anything truly worthy of being called an anti-tank gun; it had only 300 aircraft and the country was full of internal rivalries. However, the terrain was daunting. The campaign was a useful exercise for testing the mobility and durability of the Panzers but with the prospect of the Russian campaign in the near future it was an experience which their leaders might well have preferred to do without.

The campaign was simple enough. The 2nd Army took Zagreb. Kleist's *Panzergruppe* moved towards Nis and Skopje, in concert with the 12th Army (from Romania), then sent a thrust up to Belgrade. Belgrade was also the destination of the 46th Panzer Corps which reached the city on 12 April. On the next day the Corps entered Sarajevo. The Luftwaffe had, of course, added its contribution by devastating the Yugoslav cities. The Armistice, which meant a dictated peace, was signed on 17 April. Everything looked very satisfactory for the Germans but had they known it they were only beginning the Yugoslav campaign. The rest of it would be fought by guerrillas who would tie down large numbers of valuable German troops for the remainder of the war.

The campaign against Greece also began on 6 April. This lasted a little longer and the cost was higher. Most of the Greek army (fourteen divisions) was facing the Italians in Albania. Three and a half were in Macedonia facing a probable attack from Bulgaria and another three were on the Yugoslav frontier in company with an Allied army of 56,000, of which 24,000 were British. The Germans were astonished to find the Allied force there at all, for it had no hope of checking the German army for long and could have been used much more effectively in Libya. It was almost immediately outflanked by the German 12th Army which, headed by two Panzer divisions, drove down to Salonika. Soon the fourteen Greek divisions facing Albania were cut off and an attempt was made to hold the Germans in the centre of the country in what became known as the Thermopylae position. The 6th Australian Division found itself defending the famous Thermopylae pass. The Panzers drove forward relentlessly towards the Thermopylae position but the difficulties of the terrain combined with stubborn rearguard actions enabled the bulk of the Allied force to be evacuated. However, 11,000 were left behind with vast quantities of valuable equipment.

PREVIOUS PAGES Enjoying apparently endless victory, Panzers roll through the streets of Salonika upon taking Greece.

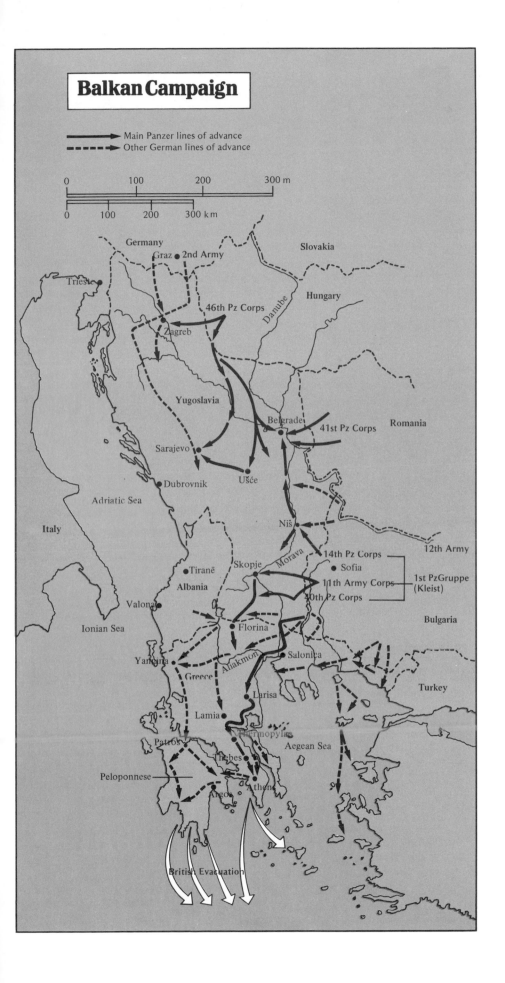

Balkan Campaign

→ Main Panzer lines of advance
⇢ Other German lines of advance

| 0 | 100 | 200 | 300 m |

| 0 | 100 | 200 | 300 km |

Germany
Graz ● 2nd Army
Slovakia

Trieste ●

Hungary

46th Pz Corps

Danube

Zagreb ●

Yugoslavia

Belgrade ●
41st Pz Corps
Romania

Sarajevo ●

Dubrovnik ●

Ušće ●

Adriatic Sea

Italy

Niš ●

12th Army

Skopje ●
Morava
14th Pz Corps
● Sofia
11th Army Corps
40th Pz Corps
1st PzGruppe (Kleist)

Tiranë ●
Albania

Valona ●
Bulgaria

Ionian Sea

Florina ●

Yannina ●
Aliakmon
Salonica ●

Greece
Turkey

Larisa ●

Lamia ●

Thermopylae
Aegean Sea

Patrós ●
Thebes ●

Peloponnese

Argos ●
Athens ●

British Evacuation

In one sense this campaign had been a triumph for the Panzers, for they had shown that they were capable of operating in difficult country which would otherwise have been considered impossible for tanks. This interesting experience might or might not prove valuable later. Apart from lost tanks and other vehicles was the unpleasant fact that two whole Panzer divisions were temporarily out of action. All their equipment now needed a thorough overhaul, and much would have to be renewed altogether. In the first stages of the drive into Russia every tank would be needed.

Surprisingly, after all this time, German production was still very poor. Tank production in 1940 was 182 a month; in 1941 it had risen to 212. This was simply not enough, for many existing tanks were obsolete, worn out, or, at best, had a limited lifetime.

In June 1941 the Germans had a total of 3,322 tanks. It was as well for their crews that they did not know that the Russians had 24,000 even though 6000 of these were in no condition to be used in a campaign, for the Panzer strength was now far short of the hoped for twenty-one divisions. Apart from the two deep in Greece there were three more which had been used in the Balkan campaign and were none the better for it mechanically. Two others had been sent to take part in the desert war.

Nevertheless, the Germans had the enormous advantage of well-trained crews and recent battle experience. This fact caused the German Chief of Staff, Halder, to estimate that the Russian campaign could be settled within ten weeks. In view of the fact that the Russians could call up an army of twelve million men, Halder's estimate seems astonishingly optimistic. But the Germans preferred to ignore lessons learned in the past of the huge numbers, vast territories and appalling weather conditions likely to be found in Russia.

The campaign, code-named 'Operation Barbarossa', began on 22 June 1941. The Russians can scarcely have been unaware that it was coming but they had done little to prepare for it. If they had made more preparations and brought more troops into the frontier area it would not have been entirely to their advantage. It was necessary that the troops which were deployed should have been better trained and more alert. The reason why too heavy a concentration of troops in the forward areas was not to Russia's advantage was linked to Panzer tactics.

In retrospect it seems extraordinary that after Panzer successes in France the men who understood armoured warfare had little say in the planning of Operation Barbarossa. The only senior officer who could be said to understand the possibilities and problems of the new type of warfare was General Friedrich von Paulus, and he was unable to make his views carry much weight. The general consensus of opinion among Panzer leaders was that the Russian campaign should be treated in the same way as the French campaign had been, that is by deep thrusts into the vital areas. The vital area of Russia, and key point, was Moscow, but it must be reached quickly. With Moscow in German hands there would be no repetition of the ill-fated Napoleonic campaign. The fact that Moscow was seven hundred miles from the German frontier was not considered to be an insuperable obstacle. Had the Germans at the time known that the Russian maps they possessed were largely unreliable, and that many of the roads over which they planned to travel had not yet been made, there might have been reservations. Nevertheless, there is reason to suppose that if the Panzers had been organized for a swift campaign and the Luftwaffe had preceded them with bombing, and accompanied them with air drops, the campaign might have ended in the predicted ten weeks.

The infantry and artillery generals who dominated the planning of Operation Barbarossa could not accept the fact that the Panzers should be allowed to outstrip infantry, artillery and supply echelons. Certainly it would be risky, even against soft opposition. But the planners' main thought was that the deep thrust principle was basically unsound in a country as large as Russia. They feared that the Russian army might slip back and be beyond the Panzer reach.

Then when the Panzers were overstretched and exhausted, as well as probably out of fuel, the Russians would hit back. Altogether it was too risky. It would be far better to emulate the Polish strategy of entering the country in great pincer movements and cutting off huge segments of the Russian army. That way the Russians would be destroyed piecemeal at the end of their long line of communications and when the Panzers, resupplied, finally thrust towards Moscow, Leningrad and Stalingrad, there would be no troops worth mentioning to stop them. This then became the agreed strategy.

But that was not quite the end of German folly. Hitler now entered the strategic ring. Just as he had demanded that Panzer strength should be doubled without regard to the availability of tanks, now he dictated strategy without regard to overall resources. He believed that Napoleon had made a vital mistake in aiming for Moscow and the error must not be repeated. More important targets were Leningrad which was a port and which had a holy significance for the Russians as having been built by Peter the Great (the city built on bones, it

Early anti-tank arguments echoed across the Steppe twenty years later when the Operation Barbarossa planners refused to acknowledge Panzer supremacy. The tanks shown here were being used to transport infantry into Russia in 1941.

73

was nicknamed) and also as the city bearing the sacred name of Lenin. The other objective was just as prestigious: Stalingrad. What greater humiliation than the capture of the city created by the present Russian leader and bearing his name? Leningrad and Stalingrad it should be; Moscow could wait until it fell like a ripe plum.

In fairness, it must be acknowledged that the reasoning behind the plan was not unsound. Leningrad was a vast workshop which, if not captured, would continue to supply the Red Army, and Stalingrad controlled the way to the Caucasus, and thus oil resources. Unfortunately for the German army, it was a plan which looked feasible – reasonably feasible – on the map but in reality contained every sort of unexpected hazard. As Kesselring bitterly pointed out, taking Moscow should have been the primary task and once that had been seized the rest of Russia could have been dealt with at leisure.

It all began very promisingly. The German forces were divided into Army Group C heading for Leningrad via Riga, Pskov and Novgorod; Army Group B heading for Moscow via Minsk and Smolensk; and Army Group A with Kiev, the Crimea and Rostov as objectives. Group C contained the 4th Panzer Group, Group B contained the 2nd and 3rd Panzer Groups and Group A contained the 1st Panzer Group. Erich von Hoeppner commanded the 4th Panzer, General Wilhelm Hoth the 3rd, Guderian the 2nd and von Kleist the 1st. Von Kleist's command included regiments which had been rushed up after the Balkan campaign and which were not wholly battleworthy.

The opening move gave high promise that all might yet be well. In Group C in the north von Manstein led the 8th Panzer Corps two hundred miles in four days and reached Dvinsk. It was a performance which suggested that had the Moscow thrust been made it would have succeeded. However, von Manstein's success also revealed some weaknesses. When tanks forced their way along roads they damaged the surface so much that it was almost impossible for their supply lorries to follow them, but when they travelled cross-country only a half-track could follow behind. Another weakness proved to be the sheer size of the area. It was possible to push past groups of Russians, taking some prisoner and

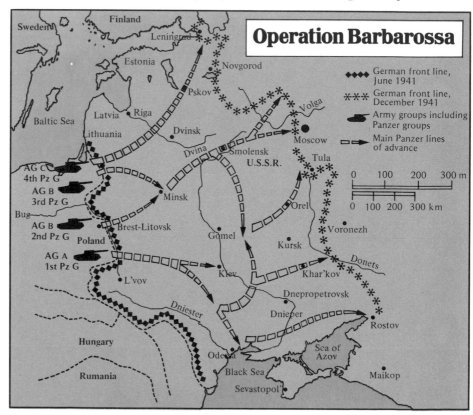

avoiding others, but the regiments which did this tended to put themselves badly out of line with their fellow regiments. An isolated regiment in hostile territory is likely to find itself in a difficult situation, particularly if it has a long and uncertain link with rear areas. When the Germans came up against the Russion 76 mm guns they were quite unable to penetrate farther. The only answer was the German 88 and that might be far away at the critical moment. The German 50 mm guns proved completely useless against the Russian KV tank which had 106 mm of armour at the front. On the other hand, the KV's 76 mm gun could pick off German field artillery while it was being set up. This was an ominous sign of future developments.

All was going well in the centre. Guderian's Panzers leapt forward to make one arm of a pincer closing on Minsk where he linked up with Hoth. Both commanders felt that the next move should be another drive forward through what appeared to be a relatively weak area. Their request to do this was refused by Halder who also vetoed a plea to let the pair close another pincer on Smolensk. Smolensk was two hundred miles farther on and its capture at this moment seemed premature to the German High Command. Guderian thought differently and once again he resorted to the 'reconnaissance' tactics he had used

Crowded battlefield in the Russian campaign, 1941

successfully in France. This time he moved forward to the Dnieper and established a bridgehead. Now not even the doubts of Halder, nor General Gunther von Kluge, whose attitude was the complete antithesis of Guderian's, could stop the drive forward. By now the Russians were reported to have lost 3000 aircraft, 1200 tanks and 600 guns. 150,000 Russians had been taken prisoner. By 10 July the Germans were on the outskirts of Smolensk. Over four hundred miles had been covered at an average speed of twenty miles a day. This was even faster than the campaigns in France where the roads had been better, and, of course, covered a greater distance. Moscow was a mere two hundred miles away. The campaign had been running for less than a month and it seemed as if the time schedule had been correctly estimated. Smolensk, however, proved to be an altogether tougher nut to crack. The Russian air force, thought to have been destroyed, now appeared with some, but not many, modern aircraft. The Russians showed a deadly accuracy with their Katyusha mortars, and the Russian soldiers, although frequently encircled, had an annoying habit of slipping out of the net and coming back to fight. Smolensk fell, but not before a rearguard action had taken its toll of the now exhausted Germans. The Panzers had now been in action for a month and no machine could be expected to stand the strain for that length of time without adequate repair and maintenance. Nevertheless, there were enough roadworthy vehicles to make Guderian cast wistful eyes in the direction of Moscow. Instead he received a direct order, said to have originated with Hitler, that he should turn south from Smolensk and close on Gomel. This would make his group the northern arm of a pincer of which the southern arm would come from Army Group A in the southern sector. If in fact this order did come from Hitler. it was probably because he sensed his own strategic planning was being thwarted and that Moscow was likely to be reached before Leningrad and Stalingrad. Even Halder saw the folly of these minor sweeps at this stage when the great prize of Moscow was within grasp. But there had been an even more disastrous interference by Hitler. He had issued instructions that all newly produced tanks should go to equip newly raised divisions. It was a senseless order because the best tanks would now be going to those least qualified to use them and the battle-scarred divisions would become less and less effective as their tank strength diminished. In September 1941 when the campaign had only been in operation for three months Panzer tank strength was already reduced by half.

Even so, the Panzers were still a force to be reckoned with, and the German army was in an excellent position. By the end of September Army Group C was on the outskirts of Leningrad, Army Group B thirty miles past Smolensk, and Army Group A at the Crimea and at Dnepropetrovsk. Success in the south had brought the valuable Ukraine into German hands. There were, however, large pockets of resistance within those areas, such as those around Odessa.

The situation in September looked so good that Hitler changed his mind once again and ordered the offensive to press forward. It began on 30 September and by nightfall on 1 October Guderian's leading Panzers had covered eighty-five miles. Another sixty-five would bring them to Moscow, although resistance was stiffening and a similar leap forward could not be expected. And then the unbelievable happened. As they were regrouping on 6 October, snow began to fall. It was not heavy, which at first seemed a blessing, but it was followed by rain. Suddenly the German army was trapped. In the north the bad weather held off a little longer but soon came there, too. It even reached the south.

The roads soon became rivers of mud in which men could sink knee-deep and tanks floundered helplessly. Wheeled vehicles could not move at all. There was no gain from leaving the roads for the fields were a mere bog. Desperate attempts to extricate vehicles merely used up valuable petrol to no avail; air supply was difficult and thus inadequate. Infantry took over from armour and where tanks could still be used regiments were at thirty per cent strength. And there was worse to come.

Moscow:100 km

...cow was within Germany's grasp but ...German High Command, displaying ...nbelievable lack of perception, argued ...t which direction the war should ..., For the men at the front, there was ...uestion.

Occasionally the rain stopped, the ground dried a little and it seemed as if the Panzers might get on the move again. Horses were brought into use; there were over 600,000 of them in the supply train but horses need feeding and looking after just like tanks and men. There was no easy solution to any problem.

In November the cold began. There was almost a cheer for the first frost for as the ground hardened it seemed that the Panzers could be pulled out of their mud holes to roll forward again. But the offensive planned for mid-November proved abortive. Starting the engines was a herculean task and once started they had to be re-started every four hours, even to go nowhere. Worse still, all the oil froze. As oil was vital to the recoil systems in the guns, these could not be used. It seemed that there was nothing which could not be frozen and rendered useless.

For the soldiers the conditions may be imagined. Anticipating a swift summer campaign, the High Command had neglected to provide warm clothing. Even so, victory might still be theirs if they could make one last effort. Desperately they tried to do so. Some troops actually reached a point in the Moscow area from which they could see the towers of the Kremlin.

That was as far as they got. There was no hope of support. There was ominous news that Rostov, captured four days earlier, had been evacuated again after Marshal Semën Timoshenko's counter-attack. On 8 December the order was issued that for the moment the Barbarossa offensive should be halted. As at the time they were beating off a counter-attack by the Russians in the Moscow area, the order must have received a cynical reception. One interesting effect of the cold was to make the telescopic sights on the tanks useless. Germany had now had 750,000 casualties, twenty-three per cent of her original strength, and 200,000 were dead, but Hitler forbade any withdrawal. To stiffen morale he sacked a number of generals. Hoeppner was dismissed as was von Rundstedt; von Bock was not dismissed but was replaced; von Brauchitsch, the Commander-in-Chief, was dismissed and Hitler appointed himself to the post. Guderian, whose views were well known, was relieved of his command. It was a cold winter indeed.

The situation on the Russian front during the winter of 1941–2 was one which those who survived it are unlikely to forget. The Germans were in serious trouble. By January some Panzer regiments had not a single usable tank. Curt orders from behind demanded that troops at the front must continue to show fighting spirit even though the general offensive was now halted. Under such conditions soldiers begin to hate their fellows in misery.

It was, of course, no easier for the Russians even though they were more accustomed to such conditions. It was one thing to endure a Russian winter when one's energies were directed to keeping warm and comfortable, but quite another to be lying in trenches in the open, exposed to frost-bite and all the other hazards of sub-zero temperature. Russian losses on all fronts had been enormous; it was said that their casualties – dead, wounded, missing or prisoners – already amounted to four and a half million. The seat of government had been moved back from Moscow although Stalin himself still lived in the capital. The army was short of much necessary equipment.

Against this there were certain factors in Russian favour. One was that further east war material was being produced as fast as the factories could turn it out. It included better tanks than the Germans possessed. The KVs and T34s proved superior to German tanks when they came into contact. There was another factor, too. When the German offensive began the policy of 'terror' was condoned by an order saying that atrocities by German troops would be dealt with at unit level only. In short, 'frightfulness' became official policy once more. It was a doubtful weapon. Russians who had encountered it felt that everything they had heard about the Germans was true and that no mercy should be expected or given. The Russians were fatalistic before; now their fatalism was tinged with a wish for revenge. It was the recipe for desperate fighting.

The Russian winter offensive achieved little. An attempt was made to give the Germans a taste of their own medicine by encircling the whole of Army Group B to the west of Moscow. Hitler ordered the Germans to stand and fight but that was clearly impossible. They retreated skilfully and had the advantage that they occupied every town and village whereas the Russians were in the open. Panzers were often fighting as infantry. As anti-freeze came through most of the tanks became mobile but now were executing pincer moves on the retreat rather than on the offensive. The Germans were shocked to find that in spite of the enormous losses the Russians had sustained there seemed to be an endless supply of reinforcements. They were raw and unskilled but the supply seemed inexhaustible. The Germans slaughtered them but still more came; they slaughtered Germans but the Germans they slaughtered were trained Panzer crews and élite front-line troops fighting under conditions hopelessly unsuitable for them, and they were not so easily replaceable. Later in the war some of the Panzer crews were mere boys.

In spite of their difficulties the Germans gradually improved their position during January and February of 1941. The cold was agonizing but a tremendous appeal campaign in Germany had induced the Germans to pack off anything they could muster in the way of warm clothing to 'the boys at the front'. The Russian offensive petered out but it left some disturbing thoughts as legacies. Even when Moscow fell, there would still be other large cities. Russia is an enormous country, eight thousand miles from west to east, and so far the Germans

The formidable Russian T34s launch into battle.

had penetrated less than one eighth of it. Even more worrying was the assessment of the Russian tanks. According to General von Mellenthin, Hitler had given orders after the French campaign that the PzKw III should have its 37 mm gun replaced by a 50 mm long high-velocity gun. The order had been 'modified' by army ordnance and the 50 mm which had been fitted was a *short* low-velocity gun. With these the Germans had found themselves in the unenviable position of confronting Russian tanks which could destroy them while they themselves were still 900 yards out of range. They were now fitting 75 mm guns with urgency but the process of adapting a tank and fitting a new gun is not one which can be accomplished easily. There is, too, an inherent danger in having too many types of gun in service. As if by magic ammunition is often dispatched to the wrong destination, as the Germans had already found on the Moscow sector. Wrong calibre ammunition had been supplied and when it was being withdrawn clogged the supply routes which were so earnestly needed for the right ammunition. There are few occurrences as damaging to morale as unloading badly-needed ammunition and finding it does not fit your guns. But the biggest headache was the T34 tank. Its design was excellent but part of its strength lay in the fact that it was made of materials of which the Germans had a limited supply. It was impossible to make replica T34s; the Germans must produce their own answer. This was partly found in the PzKw IV. In general, all German tanks were uparmoured and upgunned throughout

BELOW Even when the snow thawed in the spring of 1942, the resulting mud made the roads impassable, even for the tanks.

OPPOSITE Undaunted by the minor setback of the previous Russian winter, German troops arrive at the Eastern front in May 1942 for the second thrust into Russia.

A German tank damaged in battle is being repaired near Soldatskaja in September 1942. The only thing of which the Germans could be certain at this stage was that another Russian winter loomed ahead.

the war whenever this could be done without too great an effect on speed. The Russian T34 was the first tank employing the principle of slanted surfaces which meant that anti-tank shells would bounce off rather than penetrate. This was later imitated by the Germans when they built their Panther and Königstiger and, after the war, by all the world's tank designers.

The next big German offensive would be in the spring of 1942. Spring is late in Russia for when the snows melt the combination of melting snow and torrential rain makes movement impossible. The Germans were now becoming accustomed to such conditions, though not finding them any more palatable. In April the following directives were issued by Hitler, the Commander-in-Chief. The central front, where Army Group B faced Moscow, would remain static. The main efforts would be concentrated on Leningrad in the north and the Caucasus in the south. Once these vast industrial areas were captured that would be the end of the Russian war effort.

While the Germans were preparing for this final effort to finish the war, the Russians launched their own offensive. It turned out to be abortive and disastrous. Around Leningrad the Russians did little to relieve pressure on the city and in the south, near Kharkov, Timoshenko ran into the force which the Germans were massing ready for their own offensive. The result was that 240,000 Russians were taken prisoner.

The day of the German offensive was finally settled as 28 June 1942, almost a year since the original Operation Barbarossa. Leaving a holding force in front of Moscow, Army Group B drove south-west towards Voronezh with the aim of skirting along the southern bank of the Don and eventually reaching Stalingrad. This force would act as a screen for Army Group A which could then drive deep into the Caucasus. Their thrust would take them to Maikop where they could obtain the fuel which was ever a desperate need for their armoured fighting vehicles.

At first all went so well that this seemed a repetition of the original invasions. Near Kharkov 100,000 prisoners were taken. Hitler was not satisfied; he felt that there should have been more and replaced the commander of Army Group B. Army Group A was now deep into the Caucasus, so Hitler switched a large number of troops back to Leningrad in preparation for an offensive there. The German army was now being thinly spread over an enormous area. By September it had reached the Maikop oilfields only to find them destroyed. The Russians were still strongly entrenched in the Caucasus, and they were getting the measure of fighting the Germans without experiencing too heavy losses themselves. The 4th and 6th Panzer Divisions had reached Stalingrad but could not penetrate the city. Up in the north the German attempt to capture Leningrad had failed once more. There was also another problem which had not been foreseen. Whereas the previous winter tanks had been put out of action by mud and frost, now they were often immobilized by dust which clogged up the working parts. The German army was, however, at a high point of success in September, although Hitler was not satisfied with it. Although it had gone a long way it had not gone quite far enough. None of the three vital objectives had yet been captured, and the second winter of the war was approaching. To relieve his frustrations Hitler dismissed Halder from the post of Chief of Staff. Halder was glad to go but feared for Germany. He was not the only German general to have misgivings in the apparent hour of triumph.

5 Desert

Warfare

While the Panzers were driving deeper and deeper into Russia a very different type of warfare was taking place in North Africa. This was a campaign in which Germany did not wish to be involved but from which she could not easily extricate herself once involved. There was an important gain to be made, for if all went well the rich prize of Egypt could fall into the Axis grasp; but while Egypt remained in Allied control German armies were left with an unsatisfactory and expensive role as desert wanderers.

Germany had been drawn into Africa by the deficiencies of her Italian ally. Mussolini's declaration of war on France when Germany had already won that campaign impressed nobody. Burning to prove that Italian armies could emulate the prowess of their neighbour and ally, Mussolini ventured on further enterprises. In August 1941 he had invaded British Somaliland and followed this up by entering the western part of Egypt. His invasion of Egypt was easily checked by a small British force and he then began to pour in reinforcements. In October he decided to invade Greece. It was an unhappy move, for within two weeks the Italians were glad to retire to Albania again. In December two British divisions set to work on the Italians in Egypt; by the beginning of February they had defeated ten Italian divisions, capturing 380 tanks and 130,000 prisoners of war. Mussolini's troubles were by no means over for the British force went on to eject the Italians from Eritrea, Abyssinia and Somaliland. Before the East African campaign was over Hitler had decided that something must be done to restore Axis prestige, for if his partner continued to be defeated on such a scale it seemed likely there might be a revolution in Italy. The suppression of a national uprising was more than Hitler wished to take on at that time. He decided as a first step to try to restore Axis prestige in the Western Desert. The Italians still possessed Tripolitania (Libya) and from this point a Panzer attack could be launched. Hitler therefore dispatched Erwin Rommel, a general who had distinguished himself in the French campaign while commanding the 7th Panzer Division. Rommel's army was to consist of

PREVIOUS PAGES Rommel with the Afrika Corps staff

BELOW A German-built tank trap in the desert

two Panzer divisions. This was the nucleus of the famous Afrika Corps and it
went into action on 24 February. The Afrika Corps had little experience of
desert conditions but possessed the considerable advantage of new equipment
and a commander who was a born genius at this type of warfare. Furthermore,
Rommel was his own master for Hitler could not interfere at this distance. He
began with a swift unexpected victory, completely disorganizing the British
who had become somewhat lethargic after their easy victories over the Italians.
Furthermore the British tanks were suffering mechanically from the long
campaign they had just completed. Sand and dust halved the life of a tank in the
desert. From the first swift victory Rommel passed on to others, bewildering
and bluffing his opponents by rapid change of direction, by feints and by
sudden withdrawals. Not for nothing did he acquire the nickname 'the desert
fox'. By April the British army was partly defending Tobruk and partly guarding
the line of the Egyptian frontier. There, for the time being, Rommel had to be
content. He had done all and more than could have been expected. His task
now was to fortify his own side of the Egyptian frontier and prevent the Allies
streaming back towards Libya. While much of North Africa was in German

German map of defence at Tobruk

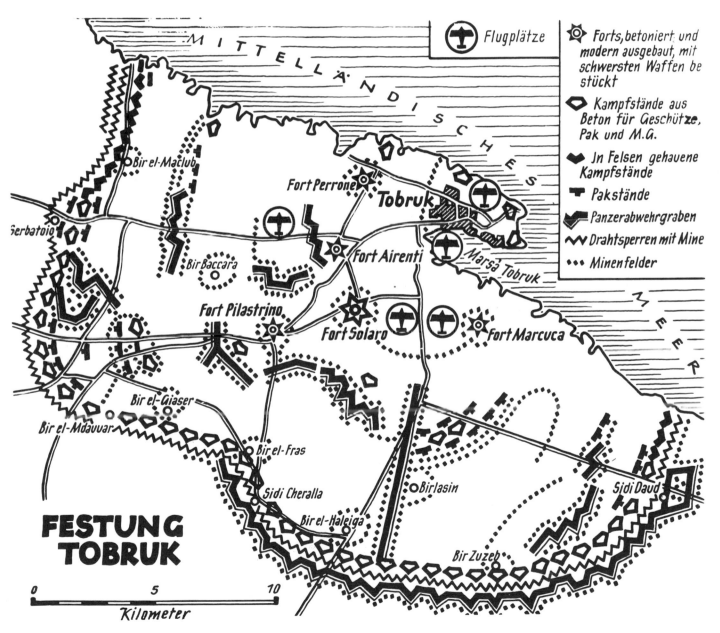

hands the Luftwaffe had bases from which to bomb Mediterranean shipping and vital Malta convoys. While biding his time, Rommel was working out plans to capture Tobruk, which was in a state of siege.

On 26 May he went into action again. There followed a series of tank battles which lasted for a month. Fortunes ebbed and flowed. First it seemed as though Rommel had split the British defence, then he was having to make a rapid retreat himself to avoid being cut off from his base. The Luftwaffe gave him full support. In the attack on Bir Hakim they flew 1300 sorties. Tank losses mounted steadily on both sides: by 12 June Rommel had 100 German and 60 Italian tanks left but the British tank strength was down to 70. These events were known as the battle of Gazala and they had resulted in a victory for Rommel. Tobruk was now open to attack. A year before Tobruk had been a strongly defended outpost, but now the defences had been robbed to assist action elsewhere and the 'fortress' was badly run down. Hastily, forces were being prepared in Egypt to save Tobruk but before they could arrive Rommel had struck. On 20 June a non-stop air and artillery bombardment began pounding Tobruk. On the twenty-first the Germans had breached the defences at ten points and the Panzers were nosing their way into the town. Counter-attacks were mounted but the garrison was very mixed and there was little co-ordination. By evening the garrison commander, who had no chance of breaking out and no prospect of holding out longer, surrendered the fortress. A party of men from the Coldstream Guards, under Major Sainthill, decided surrender was not for them and found a way through the German lines that night. The capitulation of Tobruk was a blow for the Allies and a great triumph for Rommel, who was promptly promoted to Field Marshal. Rommel, however, did not linger on the field of victory. With 44 tanks he was over the Egyptian frontier and on 23–4 June defeated the 13th Corps at Mersa Matruh. Every one of these victories was skilfully won by swift hard fighting but their organizer was now beginning to acquire a legendary fame which implied he was unbeatable. The opposing British 8th Army was worn out and in tatters; they had been outmanoeuvred and outwitted. Morale was badly affected. They had fallen back to an undistinguished stretch of sand lying between the sea and the impassable Quattara Depression. Its name was El Alamein.

The Alamein Line, as it came to be called, was in no sense a defensive position but by this time the Afrika Corps had travelled so far and done so much fighting they were in no condition to press on much farther. There was just enough British opposition to stop them if they did so. During July and August, Rommel consolidated the enormous gains of the past six months and reorganized his forces for the next plunge forward. It became obvious as he did this that time was not on his side. Allied air and sea attacks were gnawing away at his long line of communication; American troops might well be expected before the end of the year and if he did not break into the Nile valley soon he might never again have the chance to do so. In material resources the opponents were evenly matched. The British Matilda tanks ('Queens of the Desert') were tank for tank better than the PzKws, but when a Matilda came up against a well-sited German 88 mm gun, that was the end of the Matilda. On 30 August Rommel tried to break the stalemate by a swift hook at the southern end of the position at Alam Halfa. The attack petered out after a week. Three factors had defeated it. The principal one was that a new commander, a General B. L. Montgomery, had taken over command of the 8th Army on 13 August. Montgomery was convinced he could defeat Rommel and soon the rest of the 8th Army shared his belief. When Rommel sent his corps toward the Alam Halfa Ridge, it had been observed by the RAF, shelled by artillery and obstructed by deep minefields. On the ridge the 13th Corps, which he had recently defeated, was well dug in and waiting for him. After a week Rommel broke off the action. It was clear that a tactic which had worked so often before would not do so again. That was to draw out the opposing British tanks by manoeuvring in front as if searching for a gap. Then when the Allied tanks had

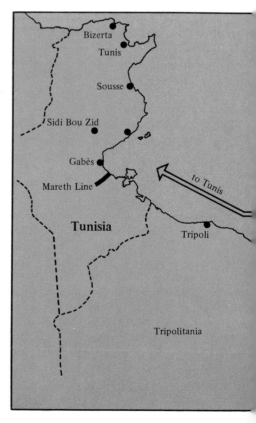

been lured forward they would be blasted to pieces by concealed anti-tank guns. This tactic had destroyed the British armour at Gazala and turned a probable German defeat into an overwhelming victory. This time the trap was set but the victims refused to enter. Instead, Rommel's force was pounded at long range by artillery and air force while Grant and Crusader tanks began creeping round the back to encircle him. It was not because he was running out of ideas that he was outmanoeuvred here. He still had plenty of ideas and was using one which had worked before and could work again. His problem was that he was running out of Panzer country. Vast stretches of the desert had been heavily mined; the Luftwaffe was no longer able to give the protection of former times and the man opposite was his equal both at shadow-boxing and roughhouse fighting.

In September Rommel returned home a sick man, with 'digestive troubles'. His command was temporarily taken over by General Georg Stumme. The Afrika Corps and its Italian allies dug themselves in along the forty-mile stretch of the Alamein Line knowing full well that the day would soon come when they would have to defend it. This defensive position was five miles deep and was heavily mined. It was held with 108,000 men of which just under half were Germans. It had 600 tanks but half of them were indifferent Italian M13s. It had twenty-four 88 mm guns, and 38 PzKw IVs with 75 mm guns. There were 345 aircraft.

Montgomery had an army which had experienced a series of stinging defeats but it now numbered 220,000 and it had 1351 tanks, of which 1000 were available on 23 October. The British were superior in artillery quantitatively but not necessarily qualitatively. Montgomery had considerable doubts about the fighting qualities of his army which was full of replacements; the 8th Army had had 80,000 casualties since its inception.

Rommel had tried to break through the Allied line and reach Cairo. Many had thought that he would succeed in doing so. However, he had failed and now the attack would come from the other direction. For a successful attack on a prepared position three to one superiority in men and materials is normally

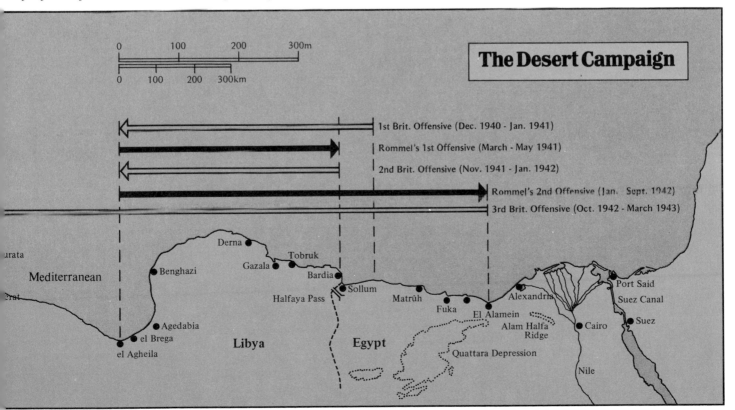

The Desert Campaign

1st Brit. Offensive (Dec. 1940 - Jan. 1941)
Rommel's 1st Offensive (March - May 1941)
2nd Brit. Offensive (Nov. 1941 - Jan. 1942)
Rommel's 2nd Offensive (Jan. - Sept. 1942)
3rd Brit. Offensive (Oct. 1942 - March 1943)

considered necessary, but such arbitrary calculations have frequently been proved to be quite wrong. Sometimes a determined attack by a small force can burrow through an extensive defence; at others a few resolute defenders can hurl back many times their own numbers. At Alamein it was difficult to calculate the odds. Montgomery had a numerical advantage but was attacking through a dangerous area. Rommel was a superb leader with an élite force but he faced a military brain as astute as his own.

Of the German Panzer leaders Rommel was the most attractive personality. He was not one of the Panzer pioneers who had fought long and hard for the establishment of this arm and whose devotion to warfare earned them contemporary admiration. Rommel came later in the field but made his mark in France. In the desert he showed such dash and originality that he appalled the German High Command. But he won battles and won them as often as not with forces inferior in numbers. Almost as bad from the point of view of the British GHQ was that he was popular even with his opponents. Directives had to be issued that the British were fighting the Germans and the Axis and not 'Rommel'. From the beginning of the Italian campaign war in the desert had been fought with a degree of chivalry. When the Afrika Corps arrived everyone expected that the atmosphere would be different, and resemble that on other fronts. But it did not change. Exasperated British commanders had to counter an attitude that it was no disgrace to be beaten by a clever chap like Rommel who looked and behaved like a gentleman.

The critical battle, by which the Allies would break through the Alamein Line, was timed for 23 October. In the open desert it was impossible to conceal the fact that preparations were being made, so deceptive plans, to disguise the direction of the coming attack, were carefully devised. A complete 'army' of canvas and tin was deployed in the southern area from which an attack might well be expected to be launched. Instead, the main thrust was in the north.

At the opening of this battle General Stumme was in command in Rommel's absence. During the first night he died of a heart attack while in the battle zone. This was an unfortunate setback for the Germans for in every battle there is usually a moment when the first thrust has lost its impetus and is vulnerable to counter-attack. This point was completely missed by the Germans. Von Thoma took over command temporarily but on 25 October Rommel arrived back. The situation was by no means resolved. The German guns and minefields had taken a heavy toll and the effort of finding a way through the latter without incurring unacceptable casualties was giving the Allies more than enough food for thought. The night of 25 October had become very confused and Montgomery, who had gone to bed, was awakened and asked if he wanted to change his plan. He stated very clearly that he did not, and went back to sleep. Divisional commanders, although not lacking in resolve before, pressed on with even more desperate determination. By the morning the 15th Panzer, which had been in the way of the attack, was much mauled. Tank losses, however, were approximately even at 200 each.

This was a moment at which the battle could be won or lost, and Rommel was undoubtedly the man for it. Knowing his force was much depleted – the 15th Panzer had only thirty-one tanks left – he decided to throw in most of his reserves and stake everything on recapturing a vital hill which had acquired the nickname of 'Kidney Ridge'. The attack went on till late on the twenty-seventh when both sides seemed exhausted. It was still anyone's battle.

Montgomery now decided to tempt Rommel. He decided on a sudden thrust on the northern flank, which, if successful, would cut off the German 164th Infantry Division and open a way through to the German rear. Rommel noted the seriousness of the situation and brought up his last reserves which were the 31st Panzer and the 90th Light Division. It was 29 October. These hurled themselves on to the Australian division making the diversionary attack, but failed to scatter it.

OPPOSITE Rommel's steady success and military genius earned respect among Axis and Allied troops alike. It was a reputation earned in France but enhanced and immortalized by his desert campaigns.

RIGHT Rommel's genius was well matched and tested against the equally outstanding General Montgomery and the British Eighth Army. With the moment in their favour, British infantry advanced to the ridge beyond the disabled German tank.

BELOW German tank troops near El Braga

BELOW Tank troops relied on a number of auxiliary units, including these armoured scout cars.

The battle had now been raging for six days. At this rate it could not go on much longer. On the night of 1 November the Allies put in a final attack with everything they could muster. It rolled forward, but not without cost from the accurate German gunnery. The Germans fell back. On 3 November Hitler sent an order saying there must be no retreat and no surrender, but on the fourth he withdrew it allowing Rommel to begin to pull away. As he did so the Allies were just beginning to break through. Not surprisingly, perhaps, they were slow off the mark and were not pursuing as they should until the sixth.

On the sixth the 'Desert Fox' played his last card – or so it seemed. Torrential rain poured over the battlefield and Rommel's line of retreat. Down the one good road went the remnants of the Afrika Corps while the Allies' attempts to cut it off were made completely abortive. Nevertheless, Rommel had lost a third of his army, a thousand guns and three-quarters of his tanks. On the retreat yet more tanks had to be abandoned through lack of fuel. By the time it reached the Libya frontier the Afrika Corps was a shadow of its former self.

In describing Alamein and other large battles in this book the emphasis is put on the contribution of tanks. This, of course, was usually one aspect of an event which had many constituent parts. Tanks, as we have seen, often paved the way to victory or averted defeat but in battle no single arm can produce victory by itself.

On 8 November the fighting in North Africa took on another dimension. A large Allied force, consisting mainly of Americans, landed in Tunisia and Algeria. Its aim was to seize vital North African ports at Algiers, Oran and Casablanca. The operation was not as easy as it might seem and there was a considerable danger that instead of acquiring a firm base for an invasion of Italy the force might find itself involved in a profitless but weakening war against the Vichy French who had fourteen divisions in the area. The Germans reacted swiftly to the landing and within a week had sent in reinforcements. They included the 10th Panzer Division and some supporting units equipped with the latest and heaviest tanks, the Tigers. The élite Hermann Goering Division was on its way. What Rommel must have thought when he learnt that these reinforcements had arrived a week after he had suffered defeat at the critical battle of Alamein is not recorded but may be imagined.

The Germans took the new threat to North Africa very seriously and soon reinforcements were pouring in at the rate of a thousand a day. Germany also overran Vichy France, that is the southern half which had not previously been occupied. It was considered vital that the new American armies should be denied an easily acquired base from which they might advance to threaten the German position in Europe. The situation in Russia was by no means all that was desired but by virtue of co-opting Hungarian, Bulgarian, Italian and other troops the Axis armies there now had numerical superiority. There were, therefore,

OPPOSITE The arrival of the Americans in North Africa awakened the Germans to the importance of sending reinforcements: Panzer IIIs being unloaded at Tripoli.

BELOW German tanks: reinforcements destined for N. Africa

The Kasserine Pass, a turning-point for Rommel

troops available for the North African theatre. Unfortunately for Rommel, but probably fortunately for the Allies, Hitler had sent out another general, Hans von Arnim, to share the command with Rommel. Rommel, not unnaturally, felt that his experience and the high rank he had been awarded entitled him to have a say in matters of high policy. He felt that holding Tripolitania was impossible and the German forces should withdraw to Tunisia. The German High Command would not listen, but by January German forces had been forced back to Tunisia. They had not retreated without giving a good account of themselves. There were some brisk tank battles at the end of 1942 before the rains made the northern sector impassable. In January there was activity in the south where the 10th, 15th and 21st Panzers were now grouped. This activity steadily increased over the month and on 14 February, the 10th and 21st Panzer delivered a swift but damaging attack on the American armoured divisions at Sidi Bou Zid. The Americans did precisely what they had been expected to do. They came back as the British had done when Rommel was teaching lessons the hard way. Thus, as the Americans came forward to grapple with the Panzers, at the critical moment the Panzers wheeled away leaving the American armour exposed to murderous cross-fire from anti-tank guns and artillery. Rommel knew exactly how to drive home such a success and pursued to the Kasserine Pass. He was then checked.

The clash of personality between Rommel and von Arnim began to operate strongly to German disadvantage. Von Arnim was experimenting wastefully in the north and, in the south, Rommel was doing what he had done so often before, making the best of meagre resources. Von Arnim lost fifty tanks in futile battles in the north during February. On 6 March Rommel decided on a swift move against the British 8th Army at Medenine. It proved to be a disaster. The British had made careful dispositions of anti-tank guns, including the new 76·2 mm, and destroyed fifty of Rommel's tanks without losing one of their own in return. However Rommel was still in a strong position on what was known as the Mareth Line. This effactually blocked the Allied route to Tunis and Bizerta, which the Allies urgently required before the invasion of Sicily could be launched in the summer. Needless to say, Hitler had demanded that Tunis should be held at all costs.

On 20 March Montgomery used the 'hook' tactics which were now an established feature of the war. He attacked the German front with the 20th Corps and then drove in behind, using the 8th Armoured Brigade, a New Zealand Division, and the Free French. Rommel fought back, using the 15th Panzer and the 90th Light Division to great effect. But the Allied advance was never completely stopped. By the twenty-ninth the Mareth Line was split open and Rommel headed back into the desert. It was his last desert battle and although he had failed to win it he extricated his force with small losses. He was then ordered home to Germany and the remainder of the battles for Tunis were fought by others. The Panzers had played a distinguished part in the North African campaign and written a new chapter in the history of armoured warfare but the ultimate cost to Germany of this action to save her Italian partner was higher than she could afford. The military axiom that strength should be concentrated and not dissipated in too many activities has been proved over and over again in history and was a fundamental of successful Panzer warfare. Yet the Germans had diverted some of their Panzer strength to Africa and men who might have made all the difference on the Russian front were now either dead or languishing in prisoner-of-war camps.

By now the war was three and a half years old. With the benefit of hindsight we tend to forget how long and dreary the war years were. Three and a half years had passed since the devastating defeat of Poland which had indicated to many that the days of long campaigns were over. France, too, was a rapidly receding memory. The realities of the present were the Russian campaign, where Stalingrad had become a battle of attrition, and southern Europe where the Allies were likely to make their next thrust. There was a danger – although apparently not an imminent one – that the Allies might reappear on the French coast taunted by the Russians into opening what was called 'the second front'.

Panzer attack at Kursk, July 1943.

6 Stalingrad

Panzers and infantry firing on a
farmhouse near Kiev in December 1943.

The events of the North African war must have seemed like a fairy story to the Panzers we left probing the outskirts of Stalingrad in 1942. Any other theatre of war than the one in which a soldier is actually fighting seems a terrestrial paradise. The besiegers of Stalingrad doubtless pondered wistfully on their fortunate comrades who fought a mobile war in a sub-tropical climate, and doubtless took their recreation with dusky girls under romantic palm trees. To the Afrika Corps with sand in everything they breathed, ate, or handled, with flies, heat and tropical disease plaguing them, the Russian front might have seemed quite comfortable. But the Russian front had never been comfortable and around Stalingrad it was soon to resemble a hell on earth.

Panzer strength, instead of increasing, was weakening. In the six months up till April 1942 the Germans had lost 2300 tanks, 500 of which were never replaced. Even more ominous was the fact that German designers and factories had been caught unawares by their Russian counterparts. The KVI tank and the T34 were better armoured and had more powerful guns. The T34 was highly manoeuvrable. If these were already available now on the battlefront what more advanced designs might the Russians have in store? Anxiety was not limited to the Panzer tank crews who found themselves confronted with superior armoured fighting vehicles; it extended right through the German army. Hitler's solution was to produce longer and heavier guns at the expense of speed. The heavy PzKw IV tank, which had been designed and produced in 1936, must now be produced in greater quantities than was previously thought necessary. Modification inevitably slowed down production. Armour was thickened and the turret reshaped to take a 75 mm gun. But more than this would be needed. There were not enough PzKw IVs – only 1000 were produced in 1942 – and not enough of any of the other models either. A much heavier tank was needed. A few prototypes had been produced in 1941 of a huge tank with armour 110 mm thick and an 88 mm gun; it weighed 55 tons and it had a road speed of 25 mph. Its cross-country speed was approximately half this. This was the formidable Tiger I. It was succeeded by the even more massive Tiger II which weighed 69·7 tons; it had the same road speed but slightly less cross-country speed and had the 88 mm gun but slightly thicker all-round armour. The Tiger II had a longer 88 mm gun than the Tiger I which gave its shells a higher velocity, increased accuracy, longer range and deeper impact. (The same was true of the Panther 75 mm gun compared with the old 75 mm gun of the PzKw IV.) Meanwhile another monster was being designed, modified and produced. This was the PzKw V or Panther. Panthers could be completed twice as fast as Tigers, so Panthers were given priority. Neither of these was quite enough of a 'land battleship' for Hitler so he demanded that yet another model should be produced. This was the Maus, which was likened to a mobile pill-box but was considered by the Panzer arm to have very limited uses as a tank. It had a 128 mm gun, 350 mm armour plate at the front, and a speed of approximately 12 mph.

Although these massive tanks had certain advantages, they had the great drawback of needing huge quantities of fuel. In the 1942 offensive Panzers had frequently been halted for lack of fuel. As the tanks gathered around Stalingrad their demands for fuel were not compensated for by any extra contribution they could make to the battle. A tank needs to keep moving even in a relatively static battle or it becomes an easy target.

In the early stages of the Stalingrad battle – in August 1941 – German momentum seemed to have slowed down. This was not because of the need to conserve fuel but was due to a feeling that the war was as good as over. A final thrust in this area would capture Stalingrad, cut off the Russians from their source of oil and deal a blow to Russian morale which would soon work through to the other key points such as Leningrad and Moscow. The end was in sight. By late August, the 14th Panzer Corps was in the northern outskirts of Stalingrad, the 6th Army was on the western side and the 4th Panzer was in the

PREVIOUS PAGES Continued fighting on the Eastern front, with Stalingrad as the much-sought prize.

Tiger, Panther, Maus

As the campaign on the Eastern front grew more intense the emphasis in tank development was on speed and mass, but unfortunately one usually had to be sacrificed for the other. The PzKw IV (above left) was in action, and the Panther (above right) and Tiger (left) went on to Kursk. The massive Maus (above) never saw action in Russia.

A knocked-out German Tiger tank, one of many which failed to break through the American, Canadian and Polish troops during the Western counter-offensive, 1944.

southern sector. However, the German army was a long way from home. Although German losses were small in comparison with those of the Russians, they still amounted to a formidable quantity. The figure of half a million dead from various causes was not one which any invading army could easily bear. In this region there were a number of Italian, Romanian and Hungarian battalions, but even with them the front the Germans were trying to cover was painfully thin. Stalin had instructed the Russians to fight for every yard of territory and this they were clearly prepared to do. This had already been noted by the 14th Panzer on its approach to the suburbs. The territory to the north of Stalingrad consisted of balkas and occasional hills. A balka is a former river bed with steep banks. One hill and one balka proved surprisingly resistant to capture. The Russians were well dug in with plenty of guns and from the hill they could observe and rake the German rear areas. The Germans dive-bombed the position with Stukas, they shelled it with 88s and they attacked it with assault troops. It held out. The original estimate was that there must be four hundred Russians in the balka, but as they held out the estimate was revised and it was decided that no less than four thousand must be there. How they were subsisting was a mystery for they had had little warning of the German approach and were not supplied by air during the siege. The Germans were intensely irritated by this unexpected and troublesome strongpoint on their line of communication and eventually launched a full assault using smoke and flame-throwers. To their surprise they found that the Russians who then surrendered numbered a thousand and that they had virtually no rations. They had been subsisting on water, grass and leaves for a month. It was an ominous portent.

Stalingrad lies on the western bank of the Volga and extends over twenty miles north to south. The centre consists of factories and the outskirts of houses, some of which at the time were made of timber. The banks of the Volga are precipitous. The 6th Army grimly began trying to fight its way in and was astonished to find that not merely every street was defended but also every house. Armoured units were of little value under such conditions. That lesson had been learned at Warsaw in 1939 but it did not prevent it being relearned at Stalingrad. It may seem surprising that powerful and terrifying monsters, as the PzKws were, could be trapped and destroyed with comparative ease, for whatever the shortcomings of the various marks of PzKw, they were a symbol of menace to those confronting them. The approach of a tank is a test of the strongest nerves. It comes in sight and is suddenly close, possibly with two or three companions. Almost as soon as it is in sight it delivers a shattering blow from its huge gun. The defender with heavy explosions around him, and perhaps a burst of flame from a *Flammenwerfer*, will need to remain very cool as he trains his anti-tank gun on the slewing, slithering monster ahead. He cannot afford to make a mistake, for if he does it may well be the last time he does.

In the streets the defender is in a better position. He knows from which direction a tank will come and sees it before it sees him. His gun is zeroed on to the target area precisely. His target arrives singly and he deals with each tank as it comes. With luck he has the advantage of height so if a tank arrives un-expectedly he may still have time to deal with it without himself being seen. Once a few tanks and vehicles have been knocked out, the street is hopelessly blocked. While attempts are made to recover tanks the defender can have a profitable time picking off the recovery team. Even the fact that he is himself frequently shelled and bombed and may be in danger of being roasted alive does not materially affect his advantage. But only desperate men will hold such positions. Military history abounds with instances when attacker and defender became locked in a struggle which neither could break off, even if the wish to do so were there. Verdun was a case in point. At Stalingrad the German armies knew that Hitler had set his mind on this target and that the alternatives were victory or death. On the Russian side the soldiers had their orders from Stalin; furthermore, they were fighting for a part of their homeland and knew that the hated German invaders were at the limit of their resources in every way.

In September the Russians were already fighting back. The 14th Panzer was battered daily by mass Russian attacks. It was the Germans who were now on the defensive. The Russian attacks were made with a combination of tanks and infantry. The Russian infantry went into action with a dogged determination which shocked the Germans. The slaughter mounted but the attacks continued. Nor were these the only problems the Germans faced. Russian artillery raked their positions day and night. On the outer perimeter the Germans were evolving new tactics for this unexpected battle. Instead of positioning themselves on the forward slopes of hills where they could observe and dominate the enemy, they retired behind the ridges; the forward areas had proved impossible to hold in the

A Russian soldier hurls a grenade at a passing German tank.

OPPOSITE Anti-tank defenses along the
Siegfried line

ABOVE Falaise pocket: RAF typhoons
attack German armour during the
Normandy breakout, August 1944.

face of concentrated Russian artillery fire followed by mass tank assaults. They withdrew to the rear of the slope and as soon as the Russians appeared on the sky-line of a ridge the Germans poured in every ounce of explosive they could muster. The ridges were soon littered with the shells of battered and burnt-out tanks but the assaults went on day after pitiless day. In spite of the mounting carnage the Russian attacks never slackened. In late September the commander of the 14th Panzer, General von Wietersheim, realized that if these attacks were kept up the Germans would soon be unable to hold them. Reinforcements were not available and he suggested the 14th Panzer should be pulled back to the west bank of the Don. The report did not find favour with the Higher Command; von Wietersheim was replaced and the 14th Panzer left in its highly vulnerable position.

Around the town of Kremenskaya the Don turns sharply north, then east, then south again, forming a loop. This had been held by a Romanian army but it had inexplicably given up a large part of it. It was an area which the Germans could well have defended and its surrender caused some dismay. However, the 48th Panzer now moved up to the area at the end of October. There was an impression in the German army that the Russians were losing heart, for their attacks on the 14th Panzer had diminished markedly in October. The case was, however, different. The Russians were preparing a massive offensive.

On 19 November it came, spearheaded by General Rokossovsky's Tank Army. The full weight of it fell on the Romanians. At the same time a similar powerful thrust was made to the south of Stalingrad and this, too, fell on a Romanian army. As they forced their way along, the Russians turned inwards, making a pincer movement which in all probability would close at Kalasch. If that happened the 14th Panzer and the 6th Army would be caught within it. However, a pincer needs strong claws if it is to contain two armies.

Clearly such a danger must be forestalled. To check the drive which was coming from the direction of Kremenskaya the 16th Panzer Division was switched south. It was too late. The Romanian army had collapsed. At the same time the southern pincer was turning rapidly upwards. To their astonishment and horror the Germans, who had concentrated their best troops into the front line for the final assault on Stalingrad, now found themselves encircled. Against the numbers the Russians seemed able to command, a German break out was going to be very difficult indeed. Also, with a line of communication as long as the Germans had, the chance of bringing up an adequate relief force seemed doubtful, to say the least. Von Paulus, having assessed the situation carefully, decided that the chances of a relief force were negligible and that the only salvation for his army was to abandon the plan to force a way into the city; they must fall back and break out before the net became too tight. They could then link up with the other armies on the Don and try the main assault later. Before he could put this plan into effect a message came from Hitler, 'Stay in your present position. Reinforcements will soon relieve and assist you.' Von Paulus had no option but to obey, whatever he may have thought privately on the matter.

The facts of the situation were not all known to the Germans but what they knew was ominous enough. The 6th Army consisted of twenty divisions. They were surrounded by sixty Russian divisions, and the latter figure could well be increased soon. There was no doubt that 280,000 Germans were firmly in a trap, for the Russians would not give way lightly. Von Paulus recalled that when he first came to Stalingrad he had been impressed by a battle for a grain elevator. It was a large building and to capture it the Germans had had to fight room to room, floor to floor. It was unlikely that the Russians would allow the Germans to escape easily, now that the odds were so heavily in their own favour.

The task of relieving the 6th Army was given to von Manstein, the architect of the French victory. He was an older man now and his reputation had grown with the years, but the task with which he was confronted was more than anyone might be expected to accomplish. His only source of troops was in the Rostov area, but to withdraw men from there would endanger von Kleist's successful thrust into the Caucasus. Von Kleist was already bitter about the way the Luftwaffe had been withdrawn from his own army and used instead to pound Stalingrad. He was also desperately short of fuel in an area famous for its oil resources. Hitler told von Kleist to stay where he was, right down by Mozdok, but withdrew the 57th Panzer Corps from his army and sent it to von Manstein. Von Kleist waited and wondered, for if the Russians broke through again they could cut his line of communication and isolate him in the Caucasus. At such a moment the 57th Panzer would be invaluable.

Nevertheless, all was not yet lost. Germany had an army which had hammered and sliced its way across Europe and most of Russia. The coming battles would be fought on the steppes, vast open rolling plains covered with snow. The Panzers were used to such terrain – now. Once the Russians were in the open the Panzers should prove more than a match for them by sheer experience and training. In order to make sure that every officer was sufficiently motivated, Hitler's reaction to any failure of Panzer attack or defence was to dismiss the commander with such speed that he did not even meet his successor. There were doubts about the ability of the Romanian army to stand up to any further strain, but time alone would show whether they were justified.

Von Manstein's relief force went into action on 12 December. The battle raged for the next twelve days. At first von Manstein had some success but towards Christmas Day it became obvious that the Russians had prepared yet another offensive and its aim was to slice through the Germans in the north of the Caucasus and cut off von Kleist's army. The Russians had so many tanks and the steppes were so large that the frightening possibility soon became a probability. Von Manstein's guns were soon lost and the chances of ever relieving von Paulus seemed hopeless. The Russians probed and forged on. But von Manstein

Manstein: assigned the thankless and hopeless task of relieving von Paulus and the Sixth Army.

was no novice at this particular aspect of the art of war. To him warfare fell into patterns, which often he arranged. As the Russians forged ahead in February 1943, von Manstein let them believe that victory was in their grasp and the fact that they themselves were overstretched was of little importance. On 20 February they discovered otherwise for then von Manstein closed the trap. Russian tanks were abandoned in their hundreds as von Manstein destroyed the Russian 6th Army and the 3rd Tank Army. Soon the thaw would come when mobile warfare would become impossible for a time, but von Manstein had struck at exactly the right moment to give the Germans time to take stock and recover. Unfortunately for Germany that did not apply to von Paulus and his unhappy 6th Army which had finally surrendered on 31 January. More details of their predicament, and the attempts to relieve them now emerged and were as follows.

The prize which the Russians won at Stalingrad exceeded their most optimistic expectations. The twenty divisions which had been encircled contained thirteen infantry divisions, three motorized divisions, one anti-aircraft division and three Panzer divisions, the 14th, 16th and 24th. In addition there were numerous headquarters with irreplaceable staff officers. There were also several regiments of Romanians and one Croat regiment.

This was a formidable number of troops to supply by air and it was soon obvious that the task was well beyond the abilities of the Luftwaffe. Every day 500 tons of supplies were needed but the best the Junkers could manage was an average of 100 tons a day. As may be imagined, even this unsatisfactory quota was not managed without crippling losses. The Russian air force was waiting for the incoming transport aircraft which was already in considerable trouble with the winter weather. Everything became desperately scarce: food, ammunition and petrol. Bread was so scarce that it was issued to front-line troops only. Horses were slaughtered to make soup and as horseflesh ran out some very strange and unpleasant ingredients were used to make a form of watery gruel. Starving men do not ask questions about the origins of a warm, greasy soup; their only query is whether they can have more of it. The steppe over which the Germans were spread was treeless. Any wood for fuel, therefore, had to come from Stalingrad itself, but as the process of fetching it used up petrol in the trucks very little could be brought. Shortage of petrol meant that tanks could not manoeuvre as they would have wished. The Russian pincer was very wide and the Germans, in spite of having the advantage of interior lines, found their perimeter so extensive that it was manned more thinly than they would have wished. Clearly, a large part of the 6th Army must still be used in the attempt to break into Stalingrad itself, but as the Russians tightened the noose it became necessary to withdraw some from the town and deploy them on the perimeter. In the early days the Russians made little attempt to harass the 6th Army, as they knew that time was on their side. In mid-December heavy snow and sub-zero temperatures made movement almost impossible. Air supply became thinner and more erratic. Most men thought and hoped that relief must be on the way. On 10 December their hopes seemed to be realized. General Hoth began an advance with the 4th Panzer Army. The plan was that when the 4th Panzer reached a point twenty miles from the city, von Paulus' 6th Army would break out. The 48th Panzer Corps would be thrown in when and where needed.

This plan, which led to the battle of the River Aksay, went seriously wrong from the start. The 4th Panzer Army was opposed by determined Russian forces whose resistance was so stubborn that what should have been a day's advance took a week. On 17 December the 4th Panzer and the 6th Army were still forty-five miles apart. At that moment Zhukov launched his great offensive, crashed through the Italians facing him and was racing forward towards Rostov.

At this critical moment Hoth had to throw a glance over his shoulder and decide what was best to do. The right decision was all too obvious. If Zhukov reached Rostov, Hoth's own 4th Panzer Army would be cut off as would the 48th Panzer and von Kleinst's army down in the Caucasus. Hoth's own resources were not exceptional, a number of his own troops were poor quality reinforcements and the Russians in front of him seemed untiring in their harassing attacks. His best unit was the 6th Panzer Division. How should he now employ it? The decision was taken for him, for von Manstein, who could see the problem even more clearly than Hoth, detached the 6th Panzer and sent it to block Zhukov. Hoth was left with a grand total of thirty-five tanks between two divisions. The 35 performed miracles: at one stage they outfought eighty Russian tanks.

The situation on 17 December was that the Germans had two bridgeheads over the River Aksay. If these could be held and widened von Paulus' 6th Army

Making mistake after mistake, heeding no one's advice, least of all that coming from the front, Hitler seized command of the Stalingrad area.

might still be relieved. The Russians, well aware of the threat, were determined that the bridgeheads should be wiped out and in consequence hurled troops on to them with increasing intensity. The battle swayed back and forth around the only notable feature – a railway ganger's house. Needless to say, it was soon destroyed but like many other houses, farms or even trees, became the central point of a mass graveyard. The fighting went on day after day, as ground was taken, lost and retaken. Curiously enough, in all this, von Paulus made no attempt to break out, possibly because his fuel supplies were now so low that his army could only perform a static role. Some of the hardest battles were on Christmas Day when the Russians had destroyed the German bridge-heads and were attempting to establish their own. On 26 December the Russians showed considerable ingenuity by improvising a bridge over two tanks, one German and one Russian, which had fallen into the river. By the time they were finally across it their opponents, the 57th Panzer Corps, had been destroyed. In just over a week's fighting an entire corps had lost so many men that it had virtually been obliterated.

There was no further hope for the 6th Army although its agony was by no

The capitulation of Sixth Army, 31 January 1943: von Paulus is taken prisoner.

means over. Unbelievably, Hitler took over command of the Stalingrad area. He had never been to Stalingrad and, of course, had no training in the conduct of operations. But he was the Chancellor, he had appointed himself supreme commander and he was Hitler. People will obey the most stupid petty laws made by incompetent politicians and minor officials. It should therefore surprise no one that Hitler was able to command the German army – which was trained to obedience – even though senior officers knew that his follies could lead only to their own destruction. He had already made the first mistake by forbidding von Paulus to withdraw while there was still time; now he would make the second and final one of trying to stage a Wagnerian finish in which nearly 300,000 Germans would fight to the last round which they would save for themselves. His generals suggested that the 6th Army was doomed and there was no point in letting it continue to be starved and frost-bitten as this would have no military effect whatever on the Russians. On 8 January the Russians offered surrender terms. They were refused, for the 6th Army did not believe Russian promises. Von Paulus was captured on 30 January, much to Hitler's fury. Hitler had just promoted him to Field Marshal and had fully expected that the Field Marshal would then shoot himself; others would presumably follow this excellent example. To Hitler's fury von Paulus saw no reason why he should take his own life to exonerate the Führer from the appalling mistake he had made in refusing permission to withdraw in the first place, for the loss of the 6th Army was not an event which could be taken in isolation. Its encirclement had indirectly led to the waste of many German lives in the relief attempts. Its loss upset the strategy of the entire campaign in that part of Russia. Finally, a sick despair began to filter through the German army that this sort of folly could happen again. If so, what next? Next in fact would be Tunisia, where another 250,000 Axis soldiers would come to the end of their personal war. But Hitler's confidence in his own prowess as a supreme commander remained unshaken.

At this time the Panzer leaders were noting with some interest that Russian tactics were developing fast. In the early stage the superior merits of T34 tanks had been partly offset by the inept way they had been handled by inexperienced crews. However, at the beginning of 1943 it was obvious the Russians had evolved a system of tactics which were disconcerting to their opponents. The Panzers had prided themselves on their ability to concentrate rapidly on a target and then without hesitation change to an entirely different point of attack where the enemy might well be taken by surprise. Now they found the Russians were doing the same, doing it as effectively, and doing it more frequently. Even more alarming was the tactical manoeuvring of the Russian infantry. The German lines were thinly manned but it was assumed that there were sufficient look-out points to note any attempted Russian incursion and prevent it. Nevertheless, the Germans were constantly being surprised by finding Russian detachments well within their own lines. Not only had they infiltrated during the night without being noticed, they had also managed to dig themselves in. Once established, a strongpoint like this was remarkably difficult to remove. Sometimes the Russians concentrated on infiltrating in a series of wedges. The Germans soon found that it was fatal to neglect even the thinnest of their penetrations, for within the next few hours the Russians would constantly reinforce and extend it. After a few days several bridgeheads would link up making serious bulges in the German lines.

While the 6th Army was reeling in agony in front of Stalingrad, von Manstein was preoccupied with the Russian breakthrough towards Rostov. In the forefront of the Russian advance was their Guard Corps. When the moment was ripe von Manstein ordered the 11th Panzer to cut them off. Isolated and without supplies at the end of a long thrust the Guard Corps was outfought and destroyed. That was the end of the immediate threat to Rostov.

But von Manstein's problems were only just beginning. Chief among them were Hitler's directives, particularly the ones which said that territory must not be given up and that armies should stand fast and fight. The lessons of the 6th Army at Stalingrad seemed to have been in vain. When von Manstein suggested abandoning Rostov, the better to destroy the main Russian offensive, Hitler at first refused permission. Although he had encouraged the Panzers and taken great delight in their triumphs in Poland and France, Hitler had an inherent distrust of this form of warfare. His ideas were based on the trench warfare of the First World War and he felt that territorial gains were too costly in terms of lives to be easily surrendered. However, von Manstein flew back to see him and obtained permission for his strategic withdrawal. During February and March von Manstein fought the battle he wanted over the type of terrain which suited it. As the Russians came forward the Panzers would retreat, even up to hundreds of miles. The Russians had a numerical superiority of eight-to-one but by the time their forces had been extended in pursuit of the apparently fleeing Panzers the Germans were able to turn and counter-attack with devastating success. In close-quarter fighting the Russian soldier was of the highest class but if caught by surprise flank attack when strung out over a long distance his reaction was often one of frightened bewilderment. Von Manstein's methodical destruction of the Russian army left the way clear for the freeing of von Kleist's army and the recapture of Kharkov. Once again it seemed as if the Germans might win the Russian war and take the prizes which had for so long eluded them. New tanks and weapons would replace those lost; the disaster of Stalingrad would be forgotten. The new Tiger Panzer was apparently a match for the massive new Joseph Stalin tank. Overall there was a mood of optimism in the German army in Russia. The fighting soldier was in no position to know that those in charge of German armaments production had regretfully decided that nothing Germany now did could prevent her losing the war.

Guderian had been restored to favour and held the appointment of Inspector-General of Armoured Troops. Panzer morale was high. What was needed now was a swift, devastating victory from an attack. The point chosen was the town of Kursk and the time was to be at the end of the spring thaw. At Kursk, which lay due north of Kharkov, the Russian line extended in a tempting bulge. Kursk

Nazi equipment destroyed at Kursk, 1943

itself was to be enveloped in a giant, devastating pincer movement of which the northern claw would be the 9th Army and the southern would be the 4th Panzer Army. The 4th Panzer Army contained eight Panzer divisions and the 9th Army contained five. May was the ideal month for the attack, but Hitler felt the risks were great and the armies should wait for the arrival of the new Panther tanks. Guderian, as a veteran tank commander, had some reservations about the new Panthers; in his experience new tanks could bring more problems than assets in the early stages. He deplored the committal of so much armour into the Kursk battle. Von Manstein, who had at first been enthusiastic, became more and more dubious as the attack was postponed and the Russians were said to be preparing defences at unprecedented speed. Hitler himself began to have doubts, but Generals Wilhelm Keitel and Kurt Zeitzler felt this would be a master-stroke and pressed for its continuance. On 4 July 1943 the operation, code-named 'Citadel', was launched.

The 4th Army contained certain units which were held in high esteem by Hitler though detested by many Germans and all their opponents. They were the divisions of the SS and were called Leibstandarte, Totenkopf and Das Reich. Of the SS more will be said later. There was also a somewhat unusual division which was known as PGD (*Panzerdivision Grossdeutschland*). It contained 180 tanks which were mostly Panthers. Its ancillary arms were abnormally strong. Excellent results were expected from the activities of the PGD. The stage was thus set for what was going to be the largest tank battle the world had ever experienced.

The terrain was not good tank country but was not entirely unfavourable. It was cornland, with sandy tracks, some villages and a few small rivers. The northern part was slightly higher than the southern. It was the sort of country-side in which troops could easily be concentrated and there was no doubt that by July the Russians were there in force. They were extremely well-camouflaged and although the Germans had made a careful aerial survey of the area the exact strength and dispositions of the Russians were still unknown. The attack began on a hot July afternoon and for a time all went well for the Germans. An unexpected misfortune occurred on the very first night in that a violent storm created a swamp where there had formerly been dry land. This, combined with intricate minefields and stubborn Russian resistance, quickly checked the assault. However, three days later, on the seventh, the Germans were moving forward again. After a day's progress, Russian resistance had stiffened so much that the German attack seemed completely halted. The PGD had sustained heavy casualties but had plenty of fight left in it. The southern claw of the pincer had made reasonable progress in that it had penetrated some twelve miles. As this sector had the pick of the tanks this was the least they had hoped for. The northern claw had been much less successful and was stopped after six miles. The new Porsche Tigers had not proved the battle-winners they had been expected to be. They were short of ammunition and they lacked machine-guns. A tank with machine-guns can deal effectively with enemy infantry, but without them becomes remarkably vulnerable. The German infantry could do little to help them. Finally, the Tigers were stopped by the Russian artillery.

The southern claw was able to move forward again on the eleventh but only after devastating attacks on the Russians by the Luftwaffe. It was obvious to many that Panzers were now being misused in this battle as foolishly as they had been at Stalingrad. But once the battle was joined there was little option but to try to go forward. By 14 July the Russians were counter-attacking heavily, in spite of numerous casualties. That in itself would not have been too serious if the German attack had retained its momentum and was heading in the right direction. The two claws were still sixty miles apart. Morale was affected by the failure of the Panthers as well as the Porsche Tigers. The Panthers seemed to catch fire too easily. It was assumed that there must be an inherent fault in their design and the realization that the new super-tanks were less effective than the ones they had replaced was a mortifying experience for their crews.

Hopes were again dashed with the destruction of the new tanks at Kursk.

Whether Operation Citadel could ever have been brought to a successful conclusion seems doubtful but the possibility was not explored because Hitler brought the operation to a halt on 14 July. Although it had become customary for the German High Command to blame many of their defeats on Hitler's directives, their criticisms do not always appear to have been justified. Kursk was a case in point. Hitler had received the news of the Allied invasion of Sicily and realized that Italy would come next. This could well prove a more immediate danger to Germany than distant battles in Russia. If the Russians came nearer to Germany, their long lines of communication would make them weaker as they advanced over the well-scorched earth. The Allies, with an entirely different logistical base, would become stronger. Von Manstein still felt he could win the battle of Kursk but it is difficult to see on what he can have been basing his reasoning. Germany could certainly not afford to lose any more tanks in that area. Nearly two-thirds of Germany's total tank strength (just over 3000) had been committed to the Kursk battle. Nearly one-third of the German tanks which had rolled forward to the attack on 4 July had been destroyed, and many others would soon need major maintenance. Germany knew full well that whatever her armies did at Kursk the Russians would respond with yet another massive offensive. That offensive could not be checked with anti-tank guns and artillery alone; it would also need tanks. Everybody needed tanks. Tanks were needed for France in case there should be another invasion there, however abortive it might prove to be. Tanks were needed in other areas of Russia apart from the Kursk salient. And tanks were certainly needed in Sicily and Italy.

Even before the end of Kursk the Russians were edging forward again. The German 9th Army fell back from Orel and Army Group B began retiring towards Smolensk. Another Russian offensive began heading for Kharkov, which fell on 14 August. Russian success was not unbroken, for periodically the

At Kursk Soviet soldiers examine a
captured German tank.

Panzers would lay a trap and inflict enormous casualties. But both the Russian High Command and, more surprisingly, the Russian soldier, seemed quite indifferent to casualties. Now it was the turn of the Germans to adopt the policy of 'scorched earth'. As they fell back towards the Dnieper they destroyed everything which could possibly be of use to the advancing Russians. By September the Germans were back on the Dnieper, and now they were becoming painfully aware that the distance between the Eastern front and Germany had shortened appreciably and dangerously. On 27 September the Russians crossed the Dnieper south of Kiev and established a bridgehead. The task of throwing them back into the river was given to the 48th Panzer Corps. To do so, the 48th Panzer hammered the bridgehead incessantly, and the Luftwaffe bombed it, but the Russians managed to hold on. As the attacks by the 48th Panzer Corps began to slacken the Russians were able to reinforce and widen the bridgehead; the 48th Panzer Corps, now much weakened in men and equipment, found itself forced to a new role. Its task was to contain the bulging bridgehead, prevent the Russians breaking out and ultimately join with expected German reinforcements to push the Russians back.

The Russians launched their assault on 16 October, prefacing it with an artillery barrage which was reminiscent of the barrages on the Western Front in 1916. Then came the infantry, assisted with good air cover. But by this time the Germans had also brought up the PGD, the 19th Panzer Division and an infantry division. Occasionally, a spearhead broke through the German defences but when this happened it was quickly eliminated by German tanks. The 48th Panzer Corps was now virtually at the end of its resources, even though on 23 October the 3rd Panzer Division came up to help. It seemed as if nothing could now save the Germans but at this point the Russian attack began to slacken. The 48th Panzer Corps looked grimly over a battlefield which bore no resemblance to the scene they had witnessed a week before. In this sector the Russians had decided that the price of victory was too high.

Elsewhere the Germans were not so happy. A victory by von Manstein in the south was offset by the loss of Kiev in the north. The loss of Kiev was a disaster but its most ominous aspect was that it was not the first objective of a Russian offensive but merely a stage. It was obvious that the German defences were too thinly spread through trying to cover too wide an area. Supplies were running short whereas on the Russian front supplies had never been so plentiful. American aid was now giving the Russians a surplus of goods they had scarcely imagined, let alone seen before. Among them were half-track vehicles, which would make the Russian infantry vastly more mobile. Not only was Germany desperately short of supplies; there was an acute shortage of manpower too. It was estimated that on all the eastern fronts the Germans were outnumbered by two-to-one. Nevertheless, in November the Germans decided to attempt to retake Kiev. Reconstituted and strengthened, the 48th Panzer Corps was to be the spearhead. It included the 7th Panzer, the SS Leibstandarte Panzer, the 1st Panzer, the 19th Panzer, the 25th Panzer and the SS Das Reich Panzer.

The Russians were surprised by this counter-attack and at first fell back in disarray. At Brussilov on 17 November resistance was much stiffer, and the Russians gave the Leibstandarte a severe mauling. By 26 November the Germans had killed many Russians, taken many prisoners and destroyed many tanks and guns. But they had not retaken Kiev and the winter rains now stopped further movement. When frost hardened the ground, the 48th Panzer made a last effort. In a series of battles the Panzers occupied themselves with inflicting as much harm on the Russians as possible, thereby to blunt the next Russian offensive. The Russian troops now were of much inferior quality to those who had fought in earlier battles; some were young and some were quite old. The Germans felt that the resources of Russian manpower were now running out and that victory might still be theirs. The view disregarded the fact that although Russian resources were limited they were nearly twice those of Germany, and Germany had other problems besides manpower.

The winter of 1943–4 brought two more disasters to German arms. In January a Russian offensive broke the siege lines around Leningrad and forced the Germans well back. In February and March another Russian offensive trapped 50,000 Germans in the Ukraine. Gradually the front was moving back from the Ukraine to Romania. In spite of the poor quality of many of the Russian troops, sheer numbers were still making them more than a match for the Germans, however great the casualties. It was said that German troops were sickened at the slaughter of so many young boys in the Russian battalions but, as the German élite units included the SS, already notorious for cold-blooded massacres of innocent and unarmed people in France, this report of German kindheartedness was received by the Allies with some scepticism.

Spring 1944 looked bad for Germany. The Allies were already at Anzio and Cassino and German armies were on the defensive on all fronts, but there was worse to come. Fuel supplies had always been a problem but while the synthetic plants were operating and Germany had control of the Romanian oilfields the main concern had been distribution. Now with the synthetic plants being bombed out of existence and the Romanian oilfields being steadily lost the day seemed to be approaching when the Panzers might be stopped altogether. The new Tigers and Panthers gave high promise that once their teething troubles were overcome they would be more than a match for opponents – but not if there was insufficient fuel to move them. Many Panzer divisions were now reduced to approximately 100 tanks, about half their normal establishment. The most favoured were the SS units who took not only the best equipment but also the best products of the training schools.

The summer of 1944 saw the Allied landings in France. The initial landing in France took place on 6 June, and seventeen days later the Russians launched a huge offensive of their own in the direction of Poland. It contained 166 divisions with corresponding supporting equipment. Almost immediately it broke

A Russian tank breaking through the German siege near Leningrad in the winter of 1943.

through the German defence at six separate points. Hitler was blamed for the subsequent consequences, for it was said that he had ordered the German armies to stand firm and not to give up ground until they were literally forced off it. Hitler was no doubt ignorant of many military matters, and unbalanced mentally as well, but he had risen to the head of the German state and in the course of so doing decided that many of the army commanders were less competent than they believed themselves to be. He may have been wrong in directing the early drives to Leningrad and Stalingrad instead of Moscow, but hindsight suggests that even if the Germans had captured Moscow they might still not have won the war. At this stage, undoubtedly, Hitler believed that the German armies on the eastern front were not making the effort which could have been expected of them. Hitler, of course, had not personally experienced three Russian winters; much of his army had. At this moment Hitler seems to have believed that the Russian penetrations could be pinched off by flank attacks. He therefore refused to allow his troops to give up ground. It is, of course, true that a deep thrust into enemy lines may well end with most of the intruders being cut off, and killed or taken prisoner, but that possibility depends somewhat on the relative strength and weakness of the two sides. On this occasion the Russians proved to be the stronger, and it was the Russians who trapped the Germans and not vice versa. The 3rd Panzer Army was isolated, the 4th was badly mauled and the 9th was completely trapped. Before the Germans could recover from these disasters they had also lost Minsk. Another 100,000 Germans were taken prisoner as a result of these operations. By the end of July it was estimated that Germany had lost 350,000 men when all dead, wounded, missing and prisoners were included. Russians were now near the borders of Germany. They were not quite near enough for the unfortunate inhabitants of Warsaw who decided the moment was ripe to throw off the German yoke and meet their liberators. Their liberators did not arrive. Instead the SS did. These were not even the Panzer SS, whose reputation was bad enough, but were a collection of sadists. The Poles fought back for nearly two months but eventually, after hideous atrocities, nine-tenths of Warsaw was completely demolished. The Russians did not arrive till the following January.

The remainder of the story on the eastern front was one long series of Russian advances with little to stop them. Czechoslovakia was overrun in March and April; and in April the Russian units also reached Berlin. The Panzers on the eastern front had fought their last battle.

German and Hungarian soldiers on their way to the front to counter the Allied counter thrust from Normandy to Berlin.

It is necessary to return to the western front which included a number of interesting Panzer actions. By comparison with the huge armies, vast spaces and enormous casualties of the eastern front, the Allied drive from Normandy to Berlin may seem a minor theatre. That was not, however, as it seemed to the Germans, who had stationed 600,000 soldiers along the 'West Wall' for just this sort of contingency. To break through, the Allies had just over half this number (thirty-seven divisions) and only eight divisions could be used in the initial landings. The balance was evened by the strength of Allied air and naval power.

Although the Germans had troops stationed along the coast from Holland to Britanny, most of them were massed between Calais and Cherbourg. They included eleven Panzer divisions and the way in which these should be used became a matter of considerable disagreement in the German High Command. The Commander-in-Chief was Field Marshal von Rundstedt and his appreciation of the situation was that his sixty divisions were attempting to cover too wide a front and should be withdrawn to the German frontier. Hitler, who had only begun the Russian offensive (Operation Barbarossa) when he had failed to cross the Channel and conquer England, regarded von Rundstedt's view with disfavour. His view was shared by Rommel who considered that an all-out attack on the Allies at the moment of landing would have entirely beneficial results. Von Rundstedt retained his command but was sharply informed that the Channel line would be held.

Disagreement followed between Rommel and von Runstedt as to the best method of repelling the landings when they occurred. Rommel believed that the Panzers should be kept close to the possible beachheads ready to attack as the Allies came ashore; von Rundstedt felt that the Panzers should be held till the Allies had established themselves and then unleashed. Rommel doubted whether the Panzers would be able to move up in the face of the attentions of the Allied air forces. Both had been encouraged to believe that the landings, when they came, would be in the Pas de Calais. In the event the Allies landed much farther west along the coast, approximately north of Caen and south of Cherbourg. Montgomery's plan was to draw the Germans into a tank battle at Caen and leave the way open for the Americans to race up to the Seine valley and trap the Germans who had come forward to the coast. In contrast to the German uncertainty over the use of their Panzers, the British 7th Armoured Division had behaved with almost mechanical precision. They secured the Arromanches beachhead, therefore making the Mulberry harbour possible. But by 10 June, four days after the landing, the German armour was ready to launch itself into the attack. Just before that happened, an Allied air strike destroyed Panzer Group West's headquarters and much of its transport.

In July there were a series of long slogging battles around Caen, involving seven Panzer divisions. Normandy had many hazards for tanks, not least of which was the *bocage*, a mixture of trees and pastures with the hedges growing on high ridges of soil. Here a tank crossing a hedge would be lifted upwards and could be shot through the belly while the guns were pointing skywards. An ingenious American, Sergeant Curtis G. Culin, Jr, found that the answer was to fix tusks to the tank so that it bored through the earth and remained level. With astonishing ingenuity and speed the Americans now fitted most of their tanks with similar tusks. They were the underwater obstacles the Germans had laid on the beaches to prevent the initial landings.

In July Rommel was injured in an air attack. Von Rundstedt was replaced by von Kluge and then von Kluge by Field Marshal Walther Model. Nevertheless, the Panzers were giving a good account of themselves, the Panthers and Tigers being more than a match for the Shermans in everything except quantity. In August the Germans launched a counter-attack, using four Panzer divisions. It almost reached Mortain, then it was checked. Before it could return it was caught in a pincer made up of Americans, Canadians and British. For five days

RIGHT A still from a captured German film showing a Tiger II in the Ardennes in December 1944

BELOW RIGHT A dead German soldier hangs over the back of an ammunition carrier in Luxembourg, 1945.

the trapped army, which included the 5th Panzer Division, was hammered relentlessly. At the end of it 10,000 were dead and 50,000 were prisoners.

With everything going so smoothly for the Allies on the western front, the Ardennes counter-attack on 16 December 1944 came as a rude shock. It was Hitler's own idea although he put von Rundstedt in charge of it. There is little doubt that the Allies were becoming complacent and the Germans were aware of the fact. The Ardennes front was weakly held: five American divisions, three of them under strength, were stretched over eighty-five miles. The Americans did not know the Ardennes very well; the Germans knew it very well indeed, for they had surveyed the area meticulously in 1940, and had fought through it with consummate skill. They probably knew it better than the local inhabitants.

The plan was carefully prepared. The Ardennes is difficult country and for an army to move successfully through it requires an efficient system of traffic and movement control. Ingeniously – and, of course, against the conventions of war – Germany infiltrated Otto Skorzeny's Panzer brigade, dressed in American uniforms. Skorzeny was a highly skilled behind-the-lines operator. He had kidnapped Mussolini and carried him off to Germany when the Allies believed that the Italian dictator was safely in their hands. Skorzeny's traffic controllers caused astonishing confusion, partly because they put up misleading direction signs and partly because they directed troops along roads where their presence would produce complete chaos. The Germans also relied on bad weather interfering with Allied air support.

The attack was delivered by the 6th SS Panzer Army in the north, the 5th Panzer Army in the centre and the 7th Army on the left, immediately north of Luxembourg. The ultimate objective of the plan was to capture Antwerp, but it was hoped that in the course of the operation four Allied armies would be destroyed (1st Canadian, 2nd British, 1st and 9th American). The initial attack was greatly assisted by fog, which helped the Germans on the ground they knew so well, bewildered the Americans who hardly knew it at all and prevented Allied air power coming to the rescue. When the fog lifted certain units found themselves face-to-face with enemy formations they previously thought were some distance away. Field-Marshal Edwin von Manteuffel commanded the 5th Panzer and advanced rapidly towards Dinant during the first four days. Farther north the 6th SS Panzer Army was much less successful, a fact attributed to its commander Dietrich being more renowned as a supporter of Hitler than as an exponent of armoured warfare. The Americans facing him, who included the 101st Airborne, might well have pointed out with justice that a soldier fights as well as his opponent allows him to fight, and in the 6th Panzer's case that was not very well.

By 22 December Allied forces were counter-attacking vigorously. The German 7th Army was in considerable trouble from attacks by the redoubtable General George Patton's 3rd Army. Elements of the 5th Panzer had to be diverted to meet this threat to its neighbour and was unable to drive forward as it wished to Dinant.

At this point von Rundstedt suggested to Hitler that the Ardennes battle should cease and the units involved in it be transferred to the eastern front where the situation was deteriorating rapidly. Hitler was determined that the apparent success of the Ardennes offensive should be continued and gave orders to that effect. However, the next few days saw the Panzers in considerable trouble. Patton took the pressure off Bastogne, which had not surrendered, and forged on towards Houffalize. By this time the Allied air force was in full operation. On the ground conditions were exacting, with ice and snow everywhere. Hitler had said that the Germans could hold their present positions but must not withdraw, but by 8 January another order was issued to withdraw.

The Ardennes offensive had been an expensive gamble for Germany. It had proved conclusively what most German generals already knew: that command of the air is even more important in armoured warfare than quantity or quality of tanks. Even though Panzer divisions included large numbers of *flakpanzers* which could produce a heavy volume of anti-aircraft fire, these were only effective against low-level attacks. Nothing was effective against a continuous torrent of bombs. However the Ardennes air battle was by no means one-sided. After a slow start the Luftwaffe gave ample support and as late as 1 January 1945 was able to destroy 200 allied aircraft on the ground. In the Ardennes battle 1600 Luftwaffe planes and 550 tanks were destroyed. The Allies had the heavier casualties in that nearly 80,000 were recorded against the German loss of 70,000 but, in addition, 50,000 Germans were made prisoner.

The Ardennes battle may well be long remembered for an unusual reason. It produced a historic answer that ranks with the terse statements of other military commanders, such as 'I came, I saw, I conquered' or '*Peccavi*'. When invited by the 5th Panzer to surrender the American forces under his command in Bastogne (which was completely surrounded), the American commander, General Anthony McAuliffe, answered with the simple reply 'Nuts'. Subsequently he became known as 'Nuts' McAuliffe.

The Panzer armies were withdrawn to fight other battles but nothing could affect the outcome of the war. Surprisingly enough, in spite of the hopelessness of their task, they went on fighting steadily to the very bitter end.

7 The Hermann Goering

Division

One other main battlefront needs to be considered in assessing the achievements and failures of the Panzers. It was the Italian front, which was a constant threat to Germany's southern flank. Italy was treated seriously by Germany, as may be appreciated from the fact that twenty-five divisions were sent there including the famous Hermann Goering Division and a number of other élite formations, including Luftwaffe ground troops. The Hermann Goering Division had already made its presence known in the battles for Sicily when it had caused considerable delays in the drive to the plain of Catania; it would be heard of again.

The division had originated as early as 1935, even before the German Air Force was officially reconstituted. It had been a 'police battalion'. Its first name was the Regiment General Goering. In 1938, 600 volunteers from the regiment became the 1 Bataillon Fallschirmjäger Regiment (1st Battalion Paratroopers). In 1939 it became part of the Luftwaffe with the objective of being an élite airborne unit. Every member was a parachutist, but as battles are not won by dropping men by parachute, but only by what they do when they arrive there, their ground training was long and thorough. They were given priority with supplies and had a good selection of arms including the Schmeisser 9 mm sub-machine-gun. Parachutists were delivered to their destination by the Junkers 88s and supplied with heavier weapons on the battlefield. The regiment was not considered sufficiently developed to be used operationally in Poland but performed useful service in 1940 in Denmark and Norway. It was also employed in France in 1940 as an anti-aircraft unit.

In the early stages of the Russian campaign the division fought both as infantry and as an anti-aircraft unit. It was claimed that within the first three months the regiment brought down 161 aircraft and destroyed 324 tanks; other successes included the capture of 11,000 prisoners.

In mid-1942 the unit was expanded again, this time to brigade strength. The unit was now made up of a Grenadier battalion, a Jäger battalion and a Flak battalion. There were of course the usual ancillary components. It became a keen rival of the Waffen SS, which was Heinrich Himmler's protegé. Goering was determined that his namesake unit should not be outshone by those of his colleagues and therefore increased the Hermann Goering Brigade to divisional strength. As the most prestigious part of German arms in 1942 was undoubtedly the Panzers, the Hermann Goering Division now became a Panzer unit. This new role involved new equipment and new training but this was completed in time for the division to be used in Tunisia. As this point it was commanded by

PREVIOUS PAGES Hermann Goering, whose division played an important role in the invasion of Italy and Sicily

Junkers 88s, invaluable auxiliary units

Generalleutnant Josef Schmid. Schmid was apparently better at reporting fictitious victories than actually winning battles, and under his command the division seems to have had heavy casualties. They were at the time under the command of von Arnim, who was an inferior commander compared to Rommel. However, in the conditions of the Tunisian fighting the armies of both Rommel and von Arnim suffered heavy casualties. Eventually what was left of the Hermann Goering division was taken prisoner with the other 240,000 Germans at the end of the North African campaign. Needless to say, the name was not allowed to go into oblivion and the Hermann Goering Division was hastily reconstituted in Sicily and Italy. It was equipped with Tiger tanks. This time it was commanded by General Conrath and had the somewhat unusual experience of taking part in a form of naval battle. Certain tanks which were close to the shore fired on American destroyers who responded quickly. This episode, combined with an infantry attack, left the unit short of about thirty tanks. As is well known, the Germans fought a gruelling withdrawal action and made the Allies pay a high price for victory. The Hermann Goering Division was prominent in all the later fighting.

By March 1944 the division was felt to be firmly re-established as an élite unit. It was therefore stationed at Livorno, from which it could be sent to any appropriate danger spot. This soon occurred when the Allies broke out from the Anzio beachhead. The division was sent to Valmontone in late May but by then the German position had deteriorated so much that in order to gain the advantage of speed the division was allowed to move by daylight. As it did so it was spotted by Allied aircraft. By the time it reached its destination its strength had been reduced by approximately half.

Nevertheless, it went straight into action. Soon its strength was down to one-third. On the very last day of May 1944 the last battalion of the division was so heavily mauled by American infantry that once again the Hermann Goering Division existed only on paper.

BELOW LEFT German tank units advancing over the mountains in Italy

BELOW SS units in Milan

A 7·5 cm anti-tank gun mounted on a
Marder II in Italy, 1943

However, the name could not be allowed to die, whatever the fate of its
members. In July 1944 there was yet another Hermann Goering Division, but
this one was not sent back to Italy but to the eastern front. As its arrival coin-
cided with the successful Russian offensive, its fate may be imagined, but it was
not completely destroyed. In October of the same year it was rebuilt once more
and even expanded. It went back into the line but was caught in a pincer move at
Elbing. This was the last disaster it had to face for henceforth it was known no
more.

Another name with a somewhat unhappy history was the Luftwaffe Field
Division. This was another creation of Goering who, not content with his
station as commander of the Luftwaffe, also wished to be influential among
ground units as well. Like the Hermann Goering Division, the Field Division
initially consisted of young men whose aspiration was to be in the air. However
the unit had the great advantage that when aircraft were short, and neither
flying nor ground personnel could be employed in the role for which they had
been trained, the Field Divisions offered an easy transition into conventional
infantry or armoured units. The Field Divisions eventually numbered twenty-
two, but only two of these, the 9th and 10th, were in Panzer Corps. Most of the
divisions were much below normal divisional strength, and usually numbered
between five and twelve thousand.

The orthodox Panzer divisions were numbered one to twenty-seven, but in
addition there were other units which had varying designations. These, of course,
were in addition to the Waffen SS Panzer units. The orthodox Panzer units
had varying lifetimes and experience. For instance, the 1st, 2nd, 3rd and 4th
took part in the fighting in Poland, as did the 10th; but the 5th, 6th and 7th
(which was commanded by Rommel), 8th and 9th began their active life in
France. Some of the divisions with higher numbers were formed in 1940, as
part of the nominal doubling of Panzer strength. Of these, the 27th had a short
life, for it was formed in 1942 but after hard experience on the Russian front was
disbanded in early 1943.

When the 16th Panzer was trapped at Stalingrad it temporarily ceased to
exist. In 1943 it was reformed in France and subsequently took part in both the
Italian and Russian campaigns. However, in April 1944, a division known as the

The PGD at the Eastern front, 1942

116th Panzer was formed from the 16th Panzer Grenadier Division. It had a brief though active life for it was engaged in the late 1944 French battles, in the Ardennes fighting and in Belgium where its active life came to an end.

The 130th division was known as the Panzer-Lehr Division. In early 1944, when German manpower resources were under heavy pressure, this division was formed from the personnel of various armoured training schools. It was very well equipped and was given the same priorities as the SS Panzers. In consequence it had 190 tanks and 40 guns. It was heavily mauled in Normandy but was re-equipped to take part in the Ardennes battle. Subsequently it fought in the withdrawal battles.

Grossdeutschland, or the PGD, had begun as an infantry regiment. Its transformation to a Panzer regiment began when it fought with Guderian's 2nd Panzer Army in Russia, becoming first a Panzer grenadier unit and then a full Panzer. It was always regarded as a prestigious unit and was certainly given every opportunity to justify its fame. It sustained heavy losses at Kursk and again on the Dnieper. Later it fought in Kurland. Elements of the division continued to fight up till March 1945.

There were other Panzer formations which were made up of reinforcements and unattached personnel in the closing stages of the war. Among them were the following.

Panzer Kurmark was formed in early 1945 and never consisted of more than brigade strength although officially it was a division. It was in action for two months but after that ceased to exist as a viable unit.

Panzer Feldherrnhalle 2 was also formed in 1945. It was based on a few survivors of the 13th Panzer.

Panzer Kurland was made up in the Kurland area when the German army was encircled and many units had been virtually destroyed. It was founded on the 14th Panzer which by then had ceased to exist.

Other Panzer divisions existed merely on paper, for as German losses mounted and established names went into captivity or oblivion, attempts were made to bolster morale by reference to new Panzer divisions. Names such as Panzer Clausewitz and Panzer Holstein suggested ample reinforcements but were only skeletal formations and paper plans.

8 Defeat

As Nazi Germany crashed to defeat in 1945 the Allied armies came across evidence which rapidly removed any admiration they might have had for hard fighting opponents. The story of the concentration camps and forced labour is well enough known but it is claimed that German armies fighting in France, Africa or Russia could scarcely be expected to know of the hideous atrocities carried out by the Nazi party, more particularly as these took place mainly in the infamous extermination camps. The excuse was that the army fought honourably and was not to blame for the excesses committed by civilian and para-military formations. This may be true but it can hardly excuse the torpedoing of unarmed passenger ships, nor the bombing of cities like Rotterdam. And, 'frightfulness' and the terrorization of refugees in Europe was deliberate policy. Undoubtedly there were many Germans who were sickened by this manner of waging war and, as is known, some generals had the courage to oppose Hitler. However, judging by the fact that Hitler stayed in power for three disastrous years when it was obvious that his policy must eventually ruin Germany, the opposition appears to have been as cowardly as it was incompetent. For all the retrospective criticism of Hitler's war strategy by the German High Command, it is clear that he was more than a match for them in personal strategy. Not least of the justified criticism of the German High Command is that of the way the Waffen SS was accepted as an élite unit. Although its Panzer divisions fought with courage and skill, the ethos of the Waffen SS should not have been accepted so easily.

PREVIOUS PAGES Hitler retained power even while Germany moved toward now inevitable defeat.

BELOW SS armoured reconnaissance vehicles in Metz, France, 1940

The Waffen Schutz-Staffeln was the military part of the Schutz-Staffeln and the term Waffen SS may be roughly translated as the 'armoured security formation' or 'defence echelons'. The SS originated as Hitler's bodyguard in the 1920s and from 1929 was commanded by Himmler. Owing to their uniforms the SS became known as 'the Blackshirts' and incorporated the Gestapo, the concentration camp guards and the extermination personnel. Originally the members were all of 'pure nordic stock' and of high physical standards but later in the war physical and ethnic standards went by the board. However, many of the less qualified members ethnically speaking were as brutal and barbarous as the earlier and more carefully selected members. It was incidentally a shock to the western world that Germany, with its cultural traditions in music, art, literature and philosophy, could produce so many utterly ruthless yet pains-takingly methodical savages.

The Waffen SS is normally dissociated from the barbarisms of the other branches of the SS but this is not correct. There was some movement between the different branches, and the behaviour of certain Waffen SS units in the field suggested an indoctrination and perhaps a natural affinity for barbaric practice. Many of the later additions to the Waffen SS were not true Panzer units but it was the intention that they should eventually be so.

The Waffen SS was only in the process of formation in 1939 when Germany attacked Poland. It already had the Leibstandarte SS Hitler which had grown from the original bodyguard of eight men in 1925 and was now an extremely important independent formation. It was under the orders of the official regular army, the Wehrmacht. It was also Hitler's official bodyguard unit. There were five other low grade Waffen SS divisions in existence at the time: the Reich; the Totenkopf; the Polizei; the Wiking and the Nord.

The Leibstandarte (which was also 1st SS Panzer) is also known as LSSAH, the AH standing for Adolf Hitler. It was equipped with PzKw IVs in France and was very anxious to show its prowess. However, when it was advancing towards Dunkirk, it was checked by a rearguard action by the Warwickshire Regiment. The defence was overwhelmed and about a hundred men were taken prisoner at Wormhout; most of them were wounded. Furious at this check, which reflected on their military reputation, the Leibstandarte disarmed its prisoners, herded them into a barn and then massacred them. There were eight survivors who had appeared to be dead.

The LSSAH which at this stage was only a regiment was expanded to division strength (about 20,000) in time for the invasion of Russia. It performed well on many occasions, particularly in the recapture of Kharkov. In 1943 it was in Italy where the behaviour of certain sections fell into the category of 'war crimes'. It returned to the Russian front, but not for long, and it reappeared in Normandy after the Allied landings. It was active in the Ardennes battles and a section of it massacred seventy-one American prisoners near Malmédy on 17 December. After the Ardennes it reappeared on the eastern front where it fought in Hungary and Austria.

Although there was no formal protest over the inclusion of the LSSAH in the Wehrmacht, there was considerable distaste for it at lower levels. Rommel despised it and ignored its attempts to win his approval. Other commanders at lower levels spoke contemptuously of its character. Its close links with Hitler ensured it the pick of the best equipment and area commanders in whose order of battle the LSSAH appeared gave it every opportunity to use everything it had. The SS Panzers all complained that where there was an especially awkward piece of fighting they were invariably sent to it. Undoubtedly this made them efficient though this may not have been the primary motive of the commanders who gave them their orders. With contempt and dislike for the SS there was some fear, for in 1940 Hitler had specifically stated that the future role of the Waffen SS was to be state police, responsible for law and order not only in conquered territories but also in Germany itself. That assignment would offer a fine opportunity to avenge real or imagined insults.

The Waffen SS advancing, 1941

In all, the Waffen SS divisions eventually numbered thirty-eight. They were as follows:

1st, LSSAH: As above.

2nd, Das Reich: As a proper Panzer division this dated from 1941. It fought at Kharkov and at Kiev and then was posted to France. On 10 June 1944 it massacred 642 French men, women and children at Oradour-sur-Glane near Limoges. It appeared in the Ardennes campaign and later fought in Hungary.

3rd, Totenkopf: This unit had a promising start in that in 1939 it was formed from concentration camp guards. It was mainly equipped with Czech weapons. In 1940 it was sharply repulsed by British units on the La Bassée Canal. Subsequently one of the company commanders (who was later hanged) ordered the massacre of one hundred unarmed prisoners from the Royal Norfolk Regiment at Le Paradis farm. The division fought at Kharkov, on the Dnieper and at Warsaw. By May 1943 it had been almost completely destroyed.

4th, Polizei Panzer Grenadier: This was formed in 1939 and was first used in the occupation of Poland, where it committed various atrocities. It was basically a security unit and operated against Tito's partisans in Yugoslavia and against Greek partisans in Greece. Atrocities committed around Larissa came to light after the war. It was put into the line in Poland in 1945 and a remnant of it was fighting in the outskirts of Berlin just before the end of the war.

5th, Wiking: This was formed in 1940 and incorporated volunteers from Belgium, Holland, Denmark and Norway although the majority of the inhabitants of these countries preferred to risk their lives fighting against their German occupiers rather than to co-operate, let alone collaborate with them. It was lightly used in Russia up till 1944 but in February 1944 was encircled near Kiev, in company with several other units. Wiking led a successful break out. It also fought well at Warsaw and at Budapest. Its reputation as a fighting unit was high but, as has been pointed out, having joined the enemy, the Wiking had a considerable interest in seeing that their former comrades did not win the war and bring them to trial.

6th, Nord: This was formed in 1941 and was defeated ignominiously in Lapland in the summer of the same year. It was re-formed and re-trained and mainly fought on the northern front. Its record was undistinguished. Its personnel were largely recruited in the Scandinavian countries.

7th, Prinz Eugen: Theoretically, this was made up of 'people of German stock' from the Balkan countries. It was mainly used against partisans in southern Europe and had a record for atrocities second to none.

8th, Florian Geyer: Although nominally a Panzer, this unsavoury unit was mainly occupied in anti-partisan activity in rear areas and operated with horses rather than tanks.

9th, Hohenstauffen: This was formed in 1942 but as most of the recruits were eighteen year olds it did not see action till 1944 on the eastern front. It was transferred to France and fought in Normandy, in the Ardennes and at Arnhem. Finally, it was sent to Hungary and surrendered in Austria to American forces.

10th, Frundsberg: This also began with young conscripts in 1943, but they saw action sooner than the Hohenstauffen did for they were blooded on the eastern front before being sent to Normandy in June 1944. Afterwards the division was at Arnhem and Budapest. It was finally overwhelmed by the Russians at Schonau. The fact that the members of these units were young did not prove the disadvantage which might have been expected. For certain combat units older men are better, but there are many military activities, such as that of a fighter pilot, where a man may well be at the peak of his efficiency when nineteen and markedly less efficient when over twenty.

11th, Nordland: Nordland was a late formation composed of Danes, Norwegians, and Hungarians. It was created in 1943 and soon began operating against partisans in Yugoslavia. It was then transferred to the Russian front and fought from Leningrad back to Berlin. Eventually the unit totally disintegrated.

12th, Hitlerjugend: This division, established in 1943, was composed of seventeen-year-old ex Hitler youth members and personnel drafted from the Leibstandarte. The Hitler youth movement was one of the most unpleasant aspects of Nazism for its members were encouraged to commit senseless cruelties on disarmed prisoners or wounded men. The division fought with fanatical zeal in Normandy but most of the first enrolment was wiped out in the Falaise pocket. Later in the year a refurbished division was in action in the Ardennes and later in Hungary and Austria. The remnants made great efforts to avoid being captured by the Russians.

13th, Handschar-Kroatische: This division was yet another which Germany was forced to raise to deal with troubles in Yugoslavia. (The conquest of Yugoslavia had proved to be more of a liability than an asset.) It was made up of Bosnian Croats who, it was hoped, would enjoy fighting Josip Tito's Christian Serbs. The unit was formed in February 1943 and showed no military ability though being well up to SS standards in atrocities against defenceless civilians. Many deserted as the Russians came nearer but a remnant remained active, and even fought in Hungary until 1945.

14th, Galizische: This regiment was formed in 1943 from Ukrainians (after the Germans had overrun that area). Their first action against the Russians proved a disaster and it was suspected then and later that they were less than wholehearted in their endeavours.

15th, Lettische Nr 1: This 'foreign legion' was composed of Latvians and Estonians who were happy to fight against the Russians although not very successful at doing so. Their worst disaster was at Danzig.

16th, Reichsfuhrer: This division, formed in 1943 in Slovenia, fought in Italy but was mainly engaged in 'security duties' which accounted for numerous defenceless and innocent Italians.

17th, Götzvon Berlichingen: This 1943 division seems to have been a national hotpotch but included a number of Belgians and Romanians. It was in action in Normandy soon after D-Day but was badly cut up at Falaise.

18th, Horst Wessel: An early 1944 division composed mainly of Hungarian volunteers. Much of its early, and ill-famed, activity was on security in Yugoslavia and Poland, but later it was sent to the line in Hungary where it sustained heavy casualties.

19th, Lettische Nr 2: This division had a brief life from mid-1944 to spring 1945. It consisted mainly of Latvians.

20th, Estnische: This unit was recruited from Estonia and operated with some success on the northern Russian front for nearly two years.

21st, Skanderberg-Albanische: This unit was formed in April 1944 from Albanians but the desertion rate was so high that it was disbanded within a year. A battle group was formed from the more reliable elements.

22nd, Freiwilligen: This was principally a Hungarian unit which had a short, unhappy life between 1944 and 1945, operating on the southern Russian front.

23rd, Kama-Kroatische: This unit was raised in Bosnia in 1944 but lasted a mere three months and was broken up to form replacements for other units.

23rd, Nederland: This unit took over the number 23 from the Kama-Kroatische when that unit came to an inglorious end. The Nederland was a Dutch-recruited unit which fought continuously on the northern Russian front until surrounded and destroyed in April 1945.

24th, Karstjager: Originally recruited from the SS Dachau depot in 1942. Subsequently used as anti-partisan in Italy but also fought against the British for a short time. Many of its members were Austrian-Germans.

25th, Hunyadi-Ungarische: A Hungarian unit which was formed in mid-1944, and which incurred heavy losses around Nuremberg.

26th, Ungarische: A mere 'paper' division that was destined to be formed in 1945.

27th, Langemarck: A Flemish division which was in action in 1944 and 1945 and lost heavily on each occasion.

28th, Wallonie: This was one of the better quality 'foreign legion' units. It contained a mixture of Walloons, French, Flemish and Spanish, and operated with some success in the northern sector of the eastern front.

29th, Russische: Generally considered the worst of the Waffen units, and usually disowned even by the others. Composed of Russians, the main activity seems to have been committing atrocities against Russian civilians. Reinforced by sadists from the German rear areas, it was mainly responsible for the Warsaw massacre in 1944.

29th, Italienische: This was an Italian unit which was mainly used for anti-partisan activity and which was given the number 29 after the commanders of the 29th (Russische) had been court-martialled and the unit disbanded.

30th, Russische: Another unsavoury unit formed from Russian defectors. Mainly used as anti-partisan in France but caught between the Maquis and the Allies in 1944.

31st, Freiwilligen: Not a true division, but a collection of Hungarians and Yugoslavs which made up a battle-group in 1944. Eliminated by the Russians.

The SS at Gdańsk, 1939

32nd, Januar: Formed in January 1945 from stragglers and fought on the retreat to Berlin.

33rd, Ungarische: The elements of this division were put in the line at Budapest in February 1945 and ceased to exist. The number was then given to the division Charlemagne-Französische, a French regiment of this name, which had fought continuously and with some success in Russia. It was soon afterwards completely wiped out near Berlin.

34th, Landstorm Nederland: A police unit of indifferent quality recruited from Dutch Nazis.

35th, Polizei Grenadier: A creation of February 1945 which was in a brief and bloodily disastrous action on the eastern front in April 1945.

36th, Waffen Grenadier: Recruited from prisons, penal battalions and throw-outs from other units. Operated in Warsaw where the record of atrocities was second to none. Subsequently sent to the front and captured by the Russians, who having learned who their prisoners were, promptly shot them all.

37th, Lutzow: A March 1945 creation which included some Hungarians.

38th, Niebelungen: Formed March 1945 from stragglers and very briefly in action.

As will be realized, some of the above units were well below divisional strength, many were not even German except for a few officers and NCOs, and all had a reputation which made them hated and despised. Some, of course, used their full equipment to excellent advantage but their fighting qualities were undoubtedly inspired by the fact that their records made death in action preferable to capture.

This account of the dregs of the Waffen SS was a far cry from the vision of a resurgent German arm which had been in the minds of the original Panzer pioneers. Those who learned of the activities of the Waffen SS in the later days of the war were horrified and occasionally demanded courts-martial. But, of course, it was the natural culmination of the theory that the end justifies the means, for the German army, and particularly the Panzers, had connived at their own destruction.

Panzer warfare had been a brilliant concept. A Panzer unit could reduce the period of a war from years to months. In Poland, France and the Balkans it did so. But the speed and ruthlessness of Panzer warfare, combined with the philosophy of those who backed it, were certain to produce a reaction. After the 'peaceful' occupation of Austria and Czechoslovakia, the Panzers were the spearhead of a brutal war against the Poles. Next on the list were Belgium, Holland and France, which all fell. But these successes bred over-confidence, and the facts of insufficient tank production were ignored. Russia was the next objective of unprovoked war and there appear to have been no inhibitions as the Panzer commanders set about this rash enterprise.

Great hopes were placed on new weapons which brought varying measures of success. But the inescapable facts were that there would never be enough tanks, nor for that matter, enough of the right sort of manpower. In the critical year 1943, Germany produced 6000 tanks, Britain produced 7500, the Russians produced 20,000 and the United States 30,000. Even the most superb quality weapons could not offset such an imbalance and overall, weapon for weapon, the Germans had no advantage.

There were, of course, other reasons for the failure of the Panzers. They fought the wrong battles at the wrong time and they occasionally underestimated their opponents, as in the Ardennes.

If one can forget the blood, filth, misery, waste and cruelty of aggressive warfare and look upon it as an art, the Panzers were a brilliant concept. But like the submarine, the dive-bomber and the policy of terror, the Panzers were certain to lose their effect because people who did not believe in such instruments were sure to band themselves together to defeat them.

'He that lives by the sword shall perish by the sword.'

OVERLEAF:
A Panther tank of the Sixth SS Panzer Division on a road near Monschau-Malmedy in the Ardennes, December 1944

Acknowledgments

The illustrations in this book are supplied by or reproduced by kind permission of the following:

Associated Press, London 20–1, 131 (both); Bavaria-Verlag, Munich 138; Bildarchiv Preussischer Kulturbesitz, Berlin 6–7, 15, 16, 17, *18–19, 22, 26–7, 29, 30–1*, 33, 46, 53, *54* (left), 56, *62*, 64, 65, 76 (above), 77, 82, 92 (above), *98–9, 102–3*, 113, 114–15, 116, 123, 124, 136, 142; Camera Press, London *58–9*; Eupra GmbH, Munich, 68–9, 81, 140; John Frost Historical Newspaper Service, London 39; Historical Research Unit, London 52, 80, 95, 105 (below), 132; Imperial War Museum, London 12 (above right & below), 32, 35 (all), 36, 37, 40–1, 42, 44–5, 47, 48, 60, 73, 84–5, 86, 87, 91, 92 (below), 92–3, 94, 96, 105 (above left & right, and centre), 128–9, 134–5; Keystone Press Agency, London 126 (below); J. G. Moore Collection, London *18, 55, 106–7, 110*; Novosti Press Agency, London 75, 79, 100–1, 118, 120, 121; Orbis Publishers, London *23, 110–11*, 130; Popperfoto, London 14; Radio Times Hulton Picture Library, London 12 (above left); Society for Cultural Relations with the USSR, London 108–9; Suddeutscher Verlag, Munich 8, 10 (both), 25, 76 (below), 133; US Army Photograph, Washington DC 126 (above); Weidenfeld Archives 57; Wiener Library, London (photographer: Derek Witte) 50–1 (both), *54* (right), *63, 110–11*; Zeitgeschichtliches Bildarchiv, Munich 13 (both), 66

All possible care has been taken in tracing the ownership of copyright material used in this book and making acknowledgment for its use. If any owner has not been acknowledged, the author and publishers apologize and will be glad of the opportunity to rectify the error

Numerals in italics indicate colour photographs

Picture research by Bridget Gascoyne
Maps compiled by Christopher Chant; drawn by Peter White

Index